Published jointly by Monmouthshire, Gloucestershire and Powys County Councils; Herefordshire Council; Wye Valley Area of Outstanding Natural Beauty; Forestry Commission

C000245211

The Wye Valley Walk is 136 miles (218 kilometres) long, and follows the river valley from Chepstow in Monmouthshire to the slopes of Plynlimon in Powys, criss-crossing the border between England and Wales. The route starts off in the dramatic limestone gorge of the southern Wye Valley and then, after passing through Ross-on-Wye, traverses the more gentle countryside of Herefordshire, before entering the rugged uplands of Powys, in mid-Wales. The walk is never very far from roads and houses although the settlements become smaller and more dispersed beyond Hay-on-Wye. It passes through several historic market towns - Chepstow, Monmouth, Ross-on-Wye, Hereford, Hay-on-Wye, Builth Wells and Rhayader, as well as many small villages and pretty hamlets. There are a few hilly stretches, but it is suitable for any reasonably fit walker who wishes to enjoy the varied landscapes and natural history of this delightful area. But please go properly prepared and refer to the section on safe walking on page 11.

Wye near Dixton

The Wye and its river banks are designated as a Site of Special Scientific Interest from the source to the mouth, one of the few British rivers to receive this designation. It is also a candidate Special Area of Conservation, which is a European designation. The relatively unpolluted waters of the river support a wide range of wildlife and the Wye is one of the most highly regarded salmon fisheries.

During the winter you are likely to see kingfishers, swans and other water birds, while in the summer months damselflies and dragonflies are common. Of the waterside mammals, the mink is most likely to be seen: the much larger otter is also present along many stretches of the river but it is secretive and rarely encountered. The limestone cliffs and pinnacles that characterise the Wye gorge are an important feature and many rock faces are not only important botanically, providing a habitat for rare and beautiful plants, but some of the cliffs also provide regular nesting sites for peregrine falcons.

Two centuries ago, the Wye Valley was known not as a refuge for wildlife, but as a centre for iron and paper production. Many of the fast flowing tributaries of the Wye were harnessed to power iron furnaces, wire works, paper mills and rolling mills for tin. Evidence of these bygone industries can be seen at Tintern and Whitebrook, but at other centres such as Redbrook, Symonds Yat and Lydbrook, very little remains. Fuel came from the abundant surrounding forests and was converted to charcoal before being used to charge the furnaces. Iron ore was brought first from the South Wales Valleys, and later from the iron mines of the Forest of Dean. Although it is difficult to imagine nowadays, the river was the major transport route for most goods, and was navigable as far as Hereford, although most goods had to be transferred to flat bottomed barges at Brockweir, just north of Tintern, then hauled manually up-river to their final destination.

From the 18th Century onwards the Lower Wye Valley also attracted fashionable 'Wye Tourists'. Many writers and artists sought out picturesque landscapes and in 1792 William Wordsworth, who loved the area, wrote his evocative poem "Lines Composed a Few Miles above Tintern Abbey" while staying in the valley.

THE MIDDLE AND UPPER REACHES OF THE WYE

North of Hereford the walk crosses the fertile flood plain of the river. This is cider apple country, which looks its best in May when the orchards are in full bloom. This is a thriving industry and many new orchards have been planted in recent years. It is also cattle country, the white-faced Herefords still being bred here. The natural beauty of the Wye Valley and its agricultural fertility have attracted several important families to settle in the area from the 18th century onwards, and the landscaped parklands that surround their imposing houses are another distinctive feature of this part of the walk.

As the route crosses the border back into Wales at Hay-on-Wye, the landscape changes again as the hills become higher and more rugged, and the river increasingly narrow and fast-flowing. As the walk draws gradually closer to the source the river is characterised by still, shallow, gravelly stretches interspersed with rocky cascades. Some walkers may be fortunate in spotting a red kite, for which mid-Wales has become famous. The agricultural methods used by local hill farmers are reflected in the landscape: the sheep spend the winters on the lower pastures close to the farmhouse, and spend the summer grazing at higher levels on the open mountains and moorlands.

Wye Valley woodland

THE WYE VALLEY AREA OF OUTSTANDING NATURAL BEAUTY

The first 52 miles (83 km) of the Wye Valley Walk go through the heart of the Wye Valley Area of Outstanding Natural Beauty (AONB). The Wye Valley AONB covers 128 square miles (326km^2) from Hereford to Chepstow and, designated in 1971, is unique among the 41 AONBs and 12 National Parks in England and Wales in being the only one to straddle the English Welsh border. The River Wye meanders majestically through this landscape, which has been host to many activities that have shaped the cultural identity of Britain.

Overlooking the Wye are myriad features that range from caves with Palaeolithic occupation, Roman and Celtic settlements, defensive structures such as hill forts, Offa's Dyke and mediaeval castles, secluded churches and reclusive monasteries, pioneering industrial communities and landscaped viewpoints that inspired some of the great British poets and writers and gave birth to the 'picturesque' movement. Tributaries cascade down side valleys to join the Wye, giving focus to settlements and power to early industries. Woodlands constitute 27% of the Wye Valley AONB and as a predominantly wooded environment, the Wye Valley is more fundamentally natural than virtually all the other AONBs and National Parks in the UK.

The primary purpose of the AONB designation is to conserve and enhance the natural beauty of the area. In pursuing the primary purpose sustainable forms of economic and social development are promoted along with quiet, informal enjoyment by the general public. AONBs share the same level of protection for the landscape and scenic beauty as National Parks. This is especially important for the 25,000 people who live and work in the Wye Valley AONB, and the estimated two million people who visit it.

The Wye Valley AONB Joint Advisory Committee is a strong partnership working with a small team of dedicated staff to keep the area outstanding for future generations. They rely on goodwill and central and local government funding to pursue the AONB objectives

NATURE CONSERVATION

The Wye is one of the most important rivers for nature conservation in Great Britain. The river was originally designated as a Site of Special Scientific Interest in 1978 and the River Wye (Lower Wye) and River Wye (Upper Wye) were renotified as SSSI in 1996, in recognition of its importance. Unlike the lower reaches of many other rivers, the Wye has not been subject to straightening, widening or deepening and remains in a relatively natural and unmodified state. The river's natural regime creates a wide diversity of features and habitats important to wildlife, such as pools, riffles, back channels, shingle bars, earth cliffs, rocks and boulders.

From its source in the Cambrian Mountains to its confluence with the Severn Estuary, the Wye changes from a rocky upland stream to a wide, meandering lowland river. This transition is marked by a natural increase in the nutrient status of the river, which is reflected by the diversity of plant species present.

The upper river is characterised by mosses, lichens and rushes, while the lower river is more diverse with beds of water crowfoot, pondweeds and water milfoil.

The river is lined by alders and willows along much of its length with oak, ash and rowan dominant on the upper steeper valley slopes. The upper reaches of the river run through permanent pasture with mixed farming predominant in the lower catchment.

The diverse nature of the Wye allows it to support a wide range of insects including caddis flies and mayflies in its upper reaches whilst further downstream freshwater pearl mussels, club-tailed dragonflies and shrimps can be found. Birds such as dippers, kingfishers and grey wagtails occur along the river's length and Daubenton's bats hunt along some sections of the river.

The river is also home to internationally important populations of fish, including brook, river and sea lamprey, allis and twaite shad, bullhead and Atlantic salmon, which spawn in the main river and its tributaries. otters are widespread in the catchment and Atlantic stream crayfish are common in some areas.

Much of the Wye's wildlife is sensitive to change and is not able to withstand pollution, modification to the river's regime or excessive disturbance.

PRACTICALITIES

USING THE GUIDE This guide has been jointly produced by the three County Councils (Monmouthshire, Herefordshire and Powys) that established and continue to maintain the route. They are supported by the Wye Valley Area of Outstanding Natural Beauty which stretches from the outskirts of Chepstow as far as Hereford and the Forestry Commission who manage large areas of land through which the route passes. The text describing the route was written by countryside officers. It has been independently checked by volunteers since the last version of the Guide appeared in 1996.

The text and maps are designed to make sure that you can follow the walk without hesitation or confusion, knowing at all times exactly where you are and what lies ahead. The walk has been separated into 42 convenient sections related to the coverage of individual maps - each map covers about 3 miles (5 kms). Route-finding information is included as well as information about features of interest along the way. Although the route is waymarked in both directions, this guide describes the walk from south to north.

Goodrich Castle

WALKING DISTANCES

FROM	TO	Distance in miles (approx)
Chepstow	Tintern	$5\frac{1}{2}$
Tintern	Redbrook	$8\frac{3}{4}$
Redbrook	Monmouth	$2\frac{1}{2}$
Monmouth	Symonds Yat	6
Symonds Yat	Welsh Bicknor	$3\frac{3}{4}$
Welsh Bicknor	Ross on Wye	8
Ross on Wye	How Caple	$6\frac{1}{4}$
How Caple	Fownhope	5
Fownhope	Hereford	$6\frac{1}{4}$
Hereford	Byford	10
Byford	Bredwardine	$4\frac{1}{2}$
Bredwardine	Hay on Wye	$8\frac{1}{2}$
Hay on Wye	Llowes	3
Llowes	Glasbury	2
Glasbury	Boughrood	$3\frac{1}{4}$
Boughrood	Erwood (Old Station)	$5\frac{1}{2}$
Erwood (Old Station)	Builth Wells	$7\frac{1}{4}$
Builth Wells	Newbridge-on-Wye	7
Newbridge-on-Wye	Llanwrthwl	$5\frac{1}{2}$
Llanwrthwl	Rhayader	4
Rhayader	Llangurig	12
Llangurig	Rhyd-y-benwch	$12\frac{1}{4}$
Rhyd-y-benwch	Llanidloes	8 (via Severn Way)

THE MAPS The large-scale maps of each section of the walk are based on the 1:25,000 scale Ordnance Survey Explorer series of maps, but features not relevant to the walk have been omitted, to make them clear and easy to use while walking.

The full list of current Ordnance Survey maps covering the route are as follows:-

Explorer OL14	**Wye Valley & Forest of Dean**
Explorer 189	**Hereford & Ross-on-Wye**
Explorer 202	**Leominster & Bromyard**
Explorer 201	**Knighton Presteigne**
Explorer OL13	**Brecon Beacons National Park (East)**
Explorer 188	**Builth Wells**
Explorer 200	**Llandrindod Wells & Elan Valley**
Explorer 214	**Llanidloes & Newtown**

PUBLIC RIGHTS OF WAY Most of the Wye Valley Walk follows public rights of way, but the land they cross is private, and there are some permissive sections of path, particularly through woodlands. Please keep to the line of the path and follow the waymarks where provided. Public rights of way are the responsibility of

1 In Monmouthshire: Corporate Director - Environment, Monmouthshire County Council, County Hall, Cwmbran NP44 2XH
Tel: 01633 644860 Fax: 01633 644800
email:francespoole@monmouthshire.gov.uk

2 In Herefordshire: Public Rights of Way Manager, Engineering Services, PO Box 234 Hereford HR1 2ZD
Tel: 01432 260573 Fax: 01432 261983
email:roberth@herefordshire.gov.uk

3 In Powys (outside the National Park):
Recreation and Countryside Services, Economic & Community Regeneration Directorate, Powys County Council, St John's Offices, Fiveways, Llandrindod Wells, Powys LD1 5ES
Tel: 01597 827567 Fax: 01597 827555
e-mail: ginnyc@powys.gov.uk

WAYMARKS The walk is marked by discs with a leaping salmon logo, which also appears on the front of this guide. There are also standard footpath waymarks with a yellow arrow or bridlepath waymarks with a blue arrow. If the path is diverted for any reason, such as maintenance after storm damage, or river bank erosion, please follow the waymarks and any temporary notices rather than the map until you are guided back on to the main route.

COUNTRY COURTESY Although you will probably not meet many people on the walk, except along some of the most popular sections, remember that the countryside is the workplace and home of the farming community. Please respect the privacy of those who live and work along the walk and do not do anything that might affect livestock, crops or farm machinery.

DOGS Please remember that dogs should follow the line of the path with you and not be allowed to roam all over the place. Be aware that they can cause alarm or distress to farm animals and wildlife, especially if they have young with them. It is an offence to allow a dog to attack or chase livestock and it is advisable always to keep a dog on a lead when walking through sheep enclosures, passing near to livestock and close to farmyards. Please also ensure that your dog is wormed regularly to prevent livestock infection.

DOGS AND CATTLE Advice for dog owners

- Be prepared for cattle to react to your presence especially when you have a dog with you.
- Move carefully and quietly and if possible walk around them.
- Remember to close gates behind you.
- Keep your dog under close control and on a short lead.

- Don't hang on to your dog if you are threatened by animals - let it go.
- Don't put yourself at risk. Find another way round and rejoin the footpath as soon as possible.
- Don't get between a cow and her calf.
- Don't panic! Most cows will stop before they reach you. If they follow, just walk on quietly.
- Don't forget to report any problems to the local authority.

SAFE WALKING Whether you intend to walk five or fifty miles it is important for your own comfort and safety to be properly equipped. Stout waterproof shoes or walking boots are essential and it is sensible to carry extra clothing. Waterproof outer wear is strongly recommended. Take a picnic and drink with you too. If you are walking alone remember to let somebody know where you are going and what time you expect to arrive at your destination. If you have one, carry a mobile phone. Like many long distance walks, the terrain along the Wye Valley Walk varies from steep, rocky sections to areas where the ground may be wet and muddy most of the year. Some parts of the path, mainly in the Chepstow to Monmouth area, are narrow with a steep drop on one side - take special care on these sections, particularly in wet or frosty weather. Other parts of the path are close to the riverbank which can be affected by flooding after heavy or sustained rainfall. In such circumstances it may be necessary to find an alternative route. A few sections of the route in Powys cross high open countryside. Most of these sections have lower level alternatives, if preferred.

For up to date local weather forecasts ring the relevant weather line:
Monmouthshire (maps 1-6): 0906 8500409
Herefordshire (maps 7-23): 0906 8500410
Powys (maps 24-42): 0906 8500414

LOCAL BUSINESSES Please try to support local businesses. Every purchase you make during your stay or on your walk will help local employment and preserve jobs in the countryside. Use shops, public houses and accommodation services along the route!

Fownhope

TOURIST INFORMATION AND ADVICE

Staff at Tourist Information Centres along the route will be pleased to give advice on local walks, attractions and accommodation. If you start the walk at Chepstow it is well worth visiting the Wye Valley exhibition in the TIC building.

Chepstow TIC, Castle Car Park, Bridge Street, Chepstow NP6 5EY
Tel: 01291 623772   Fax: 01291 628004
e-mail: chepstow.tic@monmouthshire.gov.uk

Monmouth TIC, Shire Hall, Agincourt Square,
Monmouth NP15 3DY
Tel: 01600 713899   Fax: 01600 772794
e-mail: Monmouth.tic@monmouthshire.gov.uk

Ross-on-Wye TIC, Edde Cross Street, Ross-on-Wye HR9 7BZ
Tel: 01989 562768   Fax: 01989 565057
e-mail: tic-ross@herefordshire.co.uk

Hereford TIC, 1 King Street, Hereford HR4 9BW
Tel: 01432 268430   Fax: 01432 342662
e-mail: tic-hereford@herefordshire.co.uk

Hay-on-Wye TIC, Oxford Road, Hay-on-Wye HR3 5DG
Tel: 01497 820144   Fax: 01497 820015

Builth Wells TIC, Groe Car Park, Builth Wells LD2 3BT
Tel: 01982 553307
e-mail: builtic@powys.gov.uk

Rhayader TIC, Rhayader Leisure Centre, North Street,
Rhayader LD6 5BU
Tel: 01597 810591
e-mail: rhayader.tic@powys.gov.uk

There are also off-route TICs at Llanidloes Tel: 01686 412605
and at Llandrindod Wells Tel: 01597 822600

ACCOMMODATION AND PUBLIC TRANSPORT

A separate free guide is regularly produced for the Wye Valley Walk. If you did not receive one when you purchased this guide please contact any of the Tourist Information Centres or local authorities who will be pleased to send it to you free of charge.

WALKERS QUESTIONNAIRE The local authorities who manage and maintain the Wye Valley Walk welcome your feedback - good and bad! Your comments will help us to make sure that we are providing what you, the walker, wants. If you can suggest any improvements to the route, the waymarking, or this guide, please let us know, so that we can make things better for those who will use the walk in the future. Even if you found everything in good order and the walk was a pleasure, apart from the weather or the odd blister, it would be nice to know that too. When reporting problems, please provide as much information as possible about the location, ideally with a photocopied map or grid reference.

WYE VALLEY WALK WEBSITE Visit the Official Wye Valley Walk website at www.wyevalleywalk.org for current information about the route.

Near Erwood

View from Symonds Yat Rock

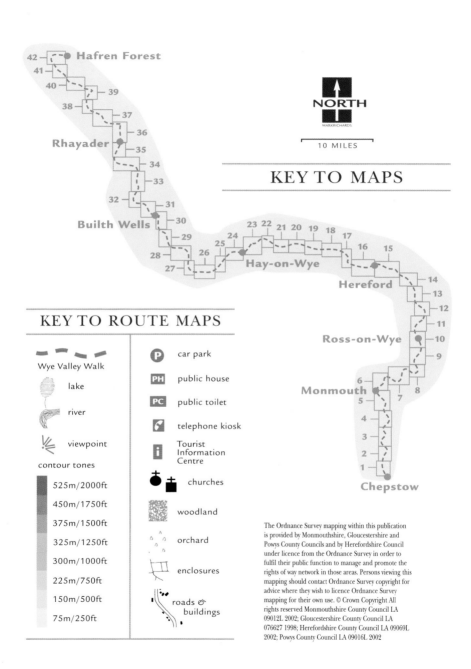

Hafren Forest

42
41
40
39
38
37
36
35 Rhayader
34
33
32 31
30 Builth Wells
29
28 27 26 25 24
23 22 21 20 19 18 17
16 15
Hay-on-Wye
Hereford 14
13
12
11
Ross-on-Wye 10
9
6
Monmouth 7 8
5
4
3
2
1
Chepstow

NORTH
MARKRICHARDS

10 MILES

KEY TO MAPS

KEY TO ROUTE MAPS

--- --- Wye Valley Walk

lake

river

viewpoint

contour tones

525m/2000ft
450m/1750ft
375m/1500ft
325m/1250ft
300m/1000ft
225m/750ft
150m/500ft
75m/250ft

P car park

PH public house

PC public toilet

telephone kiosk

i Tourist Information Centre

churches

woodland

orchard

enclosures

roads & buildings

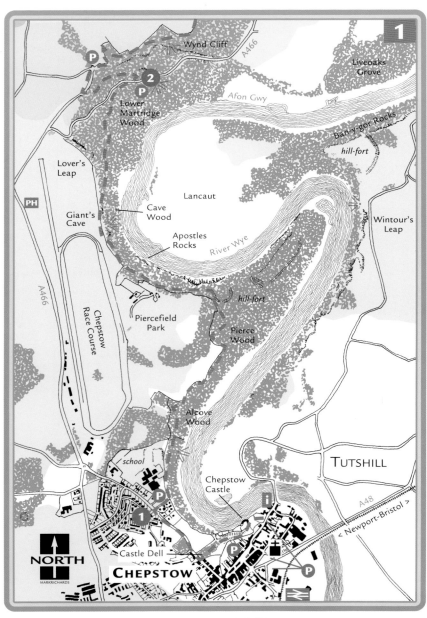

Wynd Cliff

Liveoaks Grove

P

2

Lower Martridge Wood

Afon Gwy

A466

Ban-y-gor Rocks

hill-fort

Lover's Leap

Lancaut

Cave Wood

PH

Giant's Cave

Apostles Rocks

River Wye

Wintour's Leap

A466

Chepstow Race Course

Piercefield Park

hill-fort

Pierce Wood

Alcove Wood

school

TUTSHILL

Chepstow Castle

A48

Newport-Bristol >

P

1

ℹ

P

P

NORTH

MARKRICHARDS

Castle Dell

CHEPSTOW

ONE MILE

ONE KILOMETRE

1

CHEPSTOW CASTLE TO WYND CLIFF

The map and signpost at Chepstow Castle car park marks the start of the Wye Valley Walk. *A visit to the Castle is recommended. Begun in 1067 by William Fitz Osbern, Earl of Hereford, it occupies a strategic position overlooking the Wye and is one of the few sites which illustrate the many phases of castle building in Britain.*

Before the Industrial Revolution Chepstow was an important port, until new industries founded on coal and steel resulted in the expansion of Newport and Cardiff at Chepstow's expense, but preserving the historic nature of the town.

While in Chepstow it is also worth visiting the Tourist Information Centre in the Castle car park, which houses an exhibition about walking opportunities and wildlife in the Wye Valley.

Follow "The Dell" up the left hand side of the outer castle wall following the asphalt path uphill. At the iron gates, turn right along the pavement passing "The Dell" Primary School on the right.

Chepstow Castle

1 Then take the second right turning (Wye Valley Walk fingerpost) into the grounds of Chepstow Comprehensive School and Leisure Centre. Go straight ahead to cross the car park leaving it in the left hand corner by the bottle bank. Continue between the school grounds and woodland.

At the end of the chainlink fence turn right to descend a flight of steps leading to The Alcove seat and viewpoint. *The path continues, following walks laid out by Valentine Morris, owner of the Piercefield Estate in the mid-eighteenth century. The walks, with their ten viewpoints, through woodland overlooking the Wye were popular with early tourists. Trees characteristic of ancient semi-natural woodland, such as the small leaved lime, grow in abundance here. It is probably the most outstanding area of this type of woodland in the UK today.* Continue along this well used and lovely woodland path which gradually climbs high above the Wye providing occasional glimpses of the river through the trees. Between The Alcove and the Giant's Cave there are two paths that lead up left towards the race course. Ignore both of these.

Several of Morris' features survive today, including the Grotto, a small cave decorated with stones and cinders, half hidden among the laurels, and the Giant's Cave. This is a passage cut through a rock, over the entrance to which once crouched a giant holding a boulder, although this figure has not survived the centuries. To amuse his guests Morris had some guns placed near the cave to produce an echo around the rocks.

Just after the cave ignore the left fork, taking great care not to slip on the loose rocks on the path. Cross a stream and shortly afterwards climb a flight of steps which lead to the Lower Wyndcliff car park and picnic site.

2 Cross the A466 Chepstow-Monmouth road with care following a broad track into a quarry. Here turn left (or turn right if you have the energy to tackle the 365 steps to the top!), continuing to follow it as it bends round to the right and up some steps. At Upper Wyndcliff car park turn right following the path as it continues in a gentle zig-zag up the hill. At the top is the Eagle's Nest viewpoint, the culmination of the Piercefield walks with tremendous views across the Wye 700 feet below, the Severn estuary and several counties.

Snowdrops

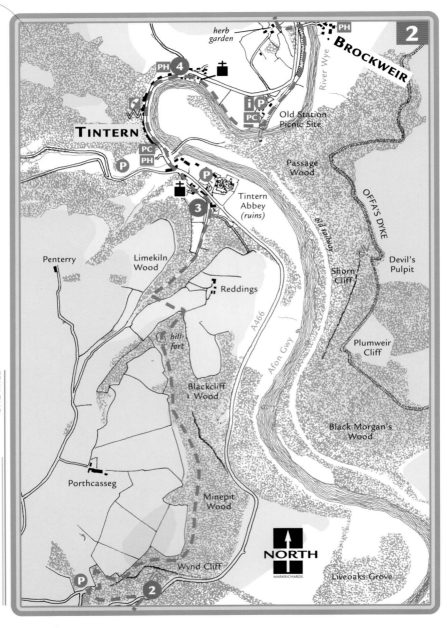

Leave the viewpoint continuing in the same direction as before, entering a beech plantation after a few hundred yards. As you leave the plantation over a prominent 'hump' note the change in soil colour underfoot as you enter Minepit Wood. Ironstone was quarried here to supply the wireworks at Tintern.

Continue on the well-used footpath through larch trees ignoring paths to left and right, and following the Wye Valley Walk waymarks. Cross the top of the Black Cliff where whitebeam (another indicator of ancient semi-natural woodland) grows in abundance. *The tree species here are diverse, including spindle, privet, small leaved lime, yew, field maple, wych elm, hazel, ash and beech.*

Eventually the path descends steeply downhill and the surface becomes

The Old Station, Tintern

Bee Orchids

rocky through a group of yew trees. The path bends to the right then left through another beech plantation to cross a stile into a field.

Turn left and then right, crossing beneath power lines keeping to the right of the pole whose top half only is visible from the stile. Cross another stile into Limekiln Wood. Continue to the left following a well used path which descends to a stream. Cross the stream and turn right along a broad, stoned old pack-horse route which may be slippery in wet weather. The track emerges in Tintern behind the Beaufort Hotel, **3** almost opposite the Abbey. Pass behind the hotel and at the next junction, carry on for the Wye Valley Walk, or for a more interesting route, follow the tarmac lane downhill to visit the Abbey.

The Abbey was founded in 1131, though the present remains date from the 13th century. The nearby Angidy Valley was important for iron production and Tintern was an industrial centre for 300 years. The Romans grew grapes here, and at least one vineyard has been re-established.

Leave the Abbey by following the riverside footpath beyond the small roundabout, after a short distance passing the site of Tintern Quay. Turn left at the village hall and turn right at the main road, following it through the village. **4** At Tintern Parva take a right, and walk through St Michael's churchyard. Pass through the gate at the other side into a field, walking along the riverside. Cross the footbridges and another field to reach the embankment of the old Wye Valley Railway Line. Turn sharp left, through a swing gate and up a flight of steps to reach the top. Turn left to reach the Old Station where there is an information centre, exhibition and refreshments available (open Easter to end of October).

Continue along the old railway line to reach a squeeze stile at the top of a flight of steps. Cross the road and turn left to cross the main Monmouth-Chepstow road with great care. **5**

Marbled White butterfly

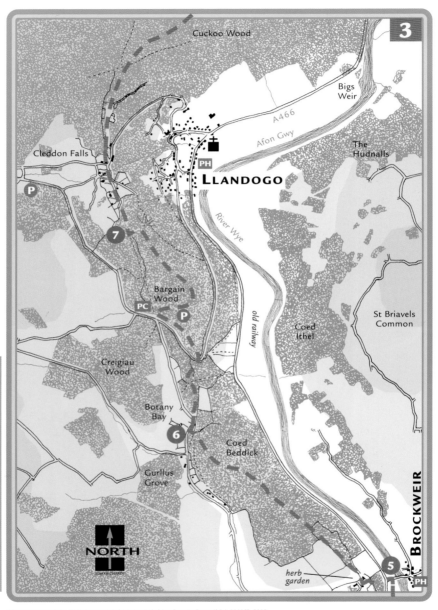

ONE MILE

ONE KILOMETRE

3

Cuckoo Wood

Bigs
Weir

A466

Afon Gwy

The
Hudnalls

Cleddon Falls

PH

LLANDOGO

P

River Wye

old railway

7

Bargain
Wood

PC

P

Coed
Ithel

St Briavels
Common

Creigiau
Wood

Botany
Bay

6

Coed
Beddick

Gurllus
Grove

NORTH

herb
garden

5

PH

BROCKWEIR

3

BROCKWEIR TO CUCKOO WOOD

The walk immediately continues up a woodland path, ascending steeply at first and then more gradually. As you approach a small barn turn sharp right up a flight of steps, crossing a track at the top. The steps are before the barn which is not obvious in the summer.

Follow this path which bears right with an orchard on the left. The path broadens into a track, entering a larch plantation and then between a thinned area on the right and mature broadleaf woodland on the left. After a short distance the path joins a wider track coming in from the left. Bear right to continue in the same direction. Notice the change underfoot from lime-stone at the start of the walk, to sandstone and quartz conglomerate. Continue in the same general direction following the waymarked path.

At the forestry turning area continue straight on past a house to reach a road. **6** Turn right leaving the road after a short distance, taking a path on the right, next to the "Scouts Botany Bay Camping and Activities Centre". Once in the wood cross a wooden

Canoeists on Wye

Marsh woundwort on bank of Wye

slatted bridge and follow the path along an avenue of conifers. After a short distance cross another two streams (sometimes dry). Cross a broad forestry track and continue in the same direction to reach a road.

Turn left and then right to cross the road and follow a waymarked path through a conifer plantation. On reaching a junction and picnic bench turn left along a well surfaced path running parallel with the road to reach Whitestones Forestry Commission picnic site after a shortish distance. At the picnic site turn right to follow the forest road towards the adventure play area.

Continue along the main track past the wooden barrier and go gently up hill through beech woods, passing three viewpoints with benches. The views of Llandogo and the Wye are superb.

7 On reaching a junction turn right along a rough forest track with a newly afforested area to the left. Continue in the same direction when the path joins another lined with stone walls. To the right there are excellent views of the village of St Briavels on the opposite hilltop. At a crossing of tracks continue in the same direction across a bridge over the Cleddon Brook just before reaching a road. Cleddon Shoots Local Nature Reserve is to the right. *It is worth a very short diversion down the steps on the right to look at the shoots, especially after wet weather.*

Cross the road following a path signed Pen-y-Fan and Wye Valley Walk. The path passes a house, ascending gradually through beech and oak woodland. The woodland floor is strewn with huge boulders of conglomerate.

As you leave the broadleaved woodland cross a wide forestry track diagonally to continue in the same direction with a conifer plantation on the left, then past a mature stand of conifers to reach a gate.

Whitestones viewpoint

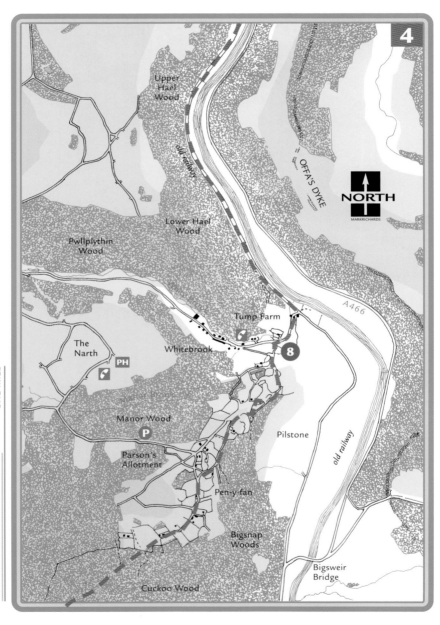

ONE MILE

ONE KILOMETRE

4

Upper
Hael
Wood

old railway

Lower Hael
Wood

Pwllplythin
Wood

OFFA'S DYKE

NORTH
MARKRICHARDS

A466

Tump Farm

The
Narth

PH

Whitebrook

8

Manor Wood

P

Pilstone

old railway

Parson's
Allotment

Pen-y-fan

Bigsnap
Woods

Bigsweir
Bridge

Cuckoo Wood

CUCKOO WOOD TO UPPER HAEL WOOD

Go through the gateway to continue in the same direction between fences. Ford or step over the stream and continue to reach a stile. Cross the stile onto a lane and continue ahead passing a white cottage typical of the community of Pen-y-Fan where each cottage has its couple of acres of land. Continue in the same direction, ignoring turns to right and left. As the lane begins to descend, providing wonderful views across the Wye Valley, fork right (signed Pen-y-Fan Green and Wye Valley Walk). Pay attention here as the path and post are not obvious in the summer. Go down this winding path, turning left at a junction to join a wider track. At the end of this track turn right down a lane alongside Pen-y-Fan Green. *Notice the weathered mounting block on the green, used for re-mounting a horse after it had been led up the steep hill from Whitebrook. There is also a seat here if you are in need of a rest.*

Continue down the lane and where it ends at a house entrance turn sharp right down a steep path signed Whitebrook Road and Wye Valley Walk. This path may look like a stream in wet weather. **8** On reaching the road turn right, proceeding carefully along the narrow

lane. *This is the Whitebrook Valley, the brook tumbles alongside the road, rushing to meet the Wye. Its power was harnessed for making wire and then paper. The remains of several of the mills can be seen on the left, converted to elegant houses.* Just past the large white farm, where the road bends sharply to the right, turn left, passing a timber barrier. *Here you join the line of the old Wye Valley Railway which closed in 1959 after 83 years of carrying passengers between Monmouth and Chepstow. The opening of the Wye Valley Railway in 1876 quickly brought the end of the former mainstay of transport up and down the valley - riverboats and trows.*

Bluebell wood near Bigsweir

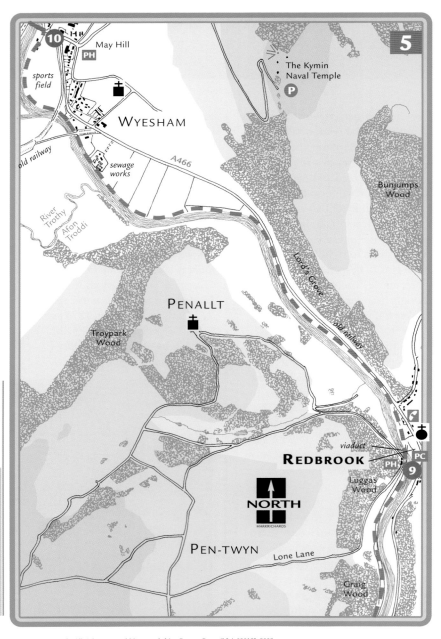

May Hill

PH

sports field

WYESHAM

old railway

sewage works

A466

River Trothy
Afon Troddi

The Kymin
Naval Temple

P

Bunjumps Wood

Lord's Grove

old railway

PENALLT

Troypark Wood

viaduct

REDBROOK

PC
PH 9

Luggas Wood

NORTH

MARKRICHARDS

PEN-TWYN

Lone Lane

Graig Wood

10

5

ONE MILE

ONE KILOMETRE

5

UPPER HAEL WOOD TO MONMOUTH (WYE BRIDGE)

Continue for about 1½ miles when a concrete forest road ascends steeply on your left. Turn sharp right over a stile on the right to reach the riverbank, and bear left continuing along this path for the last ½ mile or so to Redbrook.

Pass underneath the old iron railway bridge to reach a road opposite the "Boat Inn" well known for its extensive range of traditional ales.

9 Turn left and left again to cross the bridge. Turn left at the path on the other side, following the path round to the left and keeping left down some steps to stay close to the river. On reaching the road continue in the same direction along the pavement for about 200 yards, bearing left at the Wye Valley Walk fingerpost to reach the riverbank.

Follow the riverbank across the field and into a wood. *Notice the broken mill stones in the wood, which were manufactured at Penallt on the other side of the river and rolled down the hill to meet the trows which carried goods up and down the Wye.* Continue along the riverbank across another three large fields. Pass the sewage works and enter a narrow strip of woodland, passing beneath an

old railway viaduct and old railway bridge to enter Monmouth Boys' School Playing Field. Follow the riverbank around.

Pass through a waymarked gate by the hedge to the left of the pavilion to reach a car park. Go straight up to reach and cross the main road, turning left to cross the Wye Bridge **10**

Wye near Redbrook

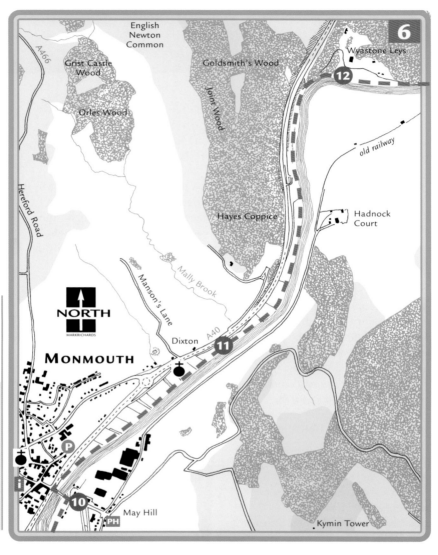

English
Newton
Common

Goldsmith's Wood

Wyastone Leys

6

12

A466

Grist Castle
Wood

Joint Wood

Orles Wood

old railway

Hayes Coppice

Hadnock
Court

Hereford Road

NORTH

MARKRICHARDS

Manson's Lane

Mally Brook

MONMOUTH

Dixton

A40

11

ONE MILE

ONE KILOMETRE

P

i

10

PH

May Hill

Kymin Tower

MONMOUTH TO WYASTONE LEYS

At the end of the bridge turn right and go down a slope to continue along the west bank of the river on a well used footpath, passing to the right of the Monmouth Rowing Club. The Monmouth School Rowing Club building is on the opposite (eastern) bank.

The attractive market town of Monmouth lies just off the route and makes an excellent stopping place on the Wye Valley Walk and the Offa's Dyke Path. The town derives its name from the Monnow river which is bridged by a unique 14th century fortified gate-house. Henry V was born in 1387 at the castle which was ruined during the Civil War. The Nelson Museum in Priory Street houses a large collection of the Admiral's love letters and gifts to Lady Hamilton. His only other connection with Monmouth was a visit in 1802 to the Naval Temple and the Roundhouse,, the whitewashed building on the summit of the 800 foot Kymin hill overlooking the town.

To continue, cross several fields along the river bank to reach the very pretty Dixton Church which is dedicated to St Peter. *Parts of the church date from Norman times, though much of it is later. Brass plates inside the church record the height of the last three great floods to inundate the church.*

After passing through the churchyard go through a gate and walk along the river bank. Turn right to cross the meandering Mally Brook by a footbridge. **11** Then continue across two large fields, keeping close to the riverbank. Cross the next stile into a wooded area, the result of a landslip that occurred during the construction of the A40 trunk road. A short distance further on you will cross the national boundary from Wales to England.

On reaching a cottage bear right over some stone steps which descend to a delightful woodland path. Cross a stile out of the woodland into a field to walk below Wyastone Leys. **12**

This is the home of Nimbus, a company producing compact discs. Nearby is a new opera house and recording studio which attracts stars from the classical music world.

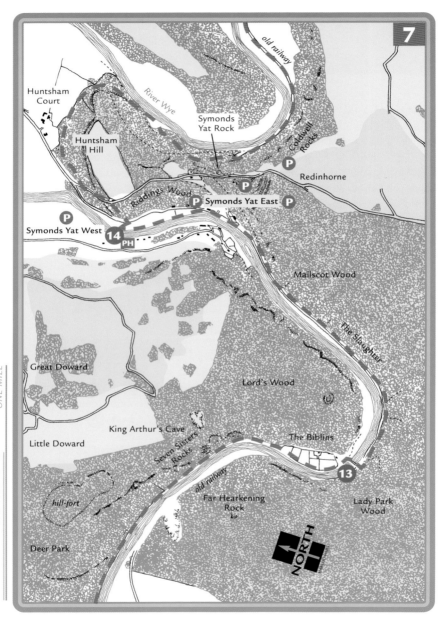

7

Huntsham Court

River Wye

Symonds Yat Rock

old railway

Coldwell Rocks

Huntsham Hill

P

Redinhorne

Riddings Wood

P

P Symonds Yat East P

P
Symonds Yat West

14
PH

Mailscot Wood

The Slaughter

Great Doward

Lord's Wood

King Arthur's Cave

Little Doward

The Biblins

Seven Sisters Rocks

13

hill-fort

old railway

Far Hearkening Rock

Lady Park Wood

NORTH

Deer Park

ONE MILE

ONE KILOMETRE

WYASTONE LEYS TO COLDWELL ROCKS

The walk enters woodland again after one large field, passing beneath the limestone cliffs and pinnacles of the Severn Sisters Rocks. *This area is of interest for various reasons. On the hill above is King Arthur's Cave where the earliest local remains of man have been discovered, together with the wild animals such as mammoth and sabre toothed cat, which shared his world. The local caves are home today to rare species of bats which maintain a stronghold in the Wye Valley. The woodland is owned by The Woodland Trust and is managed primarily for conservation.*

At the end of the wood enter a field, continuing close to the riverbank. Behind you the Seven Sisters Rocks stand out clearly against the surrounding trees. At the Biblins campsite, cross the wire suspension bridge. **13** Turn left on the other side of the river to follow a track along the line of the old GWR Railway which ran between Ross-on-Wye and Monmouth. Continue on this track, passing the rapids which are very popular with visiting canoeists, to reach Symonds Yat East. At the Forest View Hotel car park keep to the left to reach the road. After passing the Saracens Head

Biblins bridge

Above Symonds Yat East

right up into the woodland. After a few hundred yards the footpath joins a forestry track, which winds its way around Huntsham Hill, with good views northwards to Goodrich. At the top of the incline, where the track swings right, the path descends off to the left, initially down a flight of steps, through moss-covered boulders and fern clad slopes, to reach the riverbank.

The ancient woodlands here have a distinctly primeval feel to them. A little further on, as you cross a clearing, Symonds Yat Rock becomes visible on the skyline ahead of you. Continue along the river bank.

public house, the route turns left into the car park and campsite, and then follows the riverbank continuing through into the field. On reaching the ferry point **14** turn right across the field, then left along the road for 40 yards, before taking the path right, up into the woodland.

There is a large outcrop of quartz conglomerate above the path, where it emerges on the next road. This rock consists of small pebbles of quartz and igneous rock embedded in a naturally formed sandy cement.

Turn left down the road here for 70 yards and then again take the path

Eventually the path climbs back up through the woodland to rejoin the forestry track. Turn left here. At the bottom of the slope the track rejoins the old railway line. *The bricked up entrance to a railway tunnel can be seen on the right. This passes beneath the hill to Symonds Yat East.*

The footpath continues along the track. *Approximately 100 yards further on there is an optional detour up to Symonds Yat Rock. This is a stiff climb, rewarded by spectacular views on a clear day.*

View from Huntsham Hill

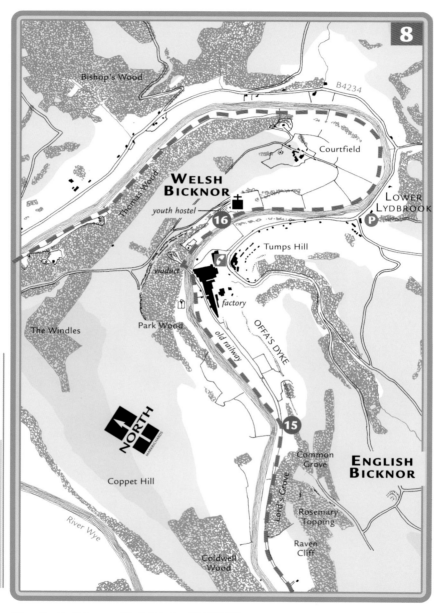

Bishop's Wood

B4234

Courtfield

WELSH BICKNOR

Thomas Wood

youth hostel

16

LOWER LYDBROOK

P

Tumps Hill

viaduct

factory

old railway

OFFA'S DYKE

The Windles

Park Wood

NORTH

15

Common Grove

ENGLISH BICKNOR

Coppet Hill

Lord's Grove

Rosemary Topping

River Wye

Raven Cliff

Coldwell Wood

ONE MILE

ONE KILOMETRE

8

COLDWELL ROCKS TO THOMAS WOOD

Shortly the path emerges into a riverside meadow and continues along the trackway, a little way back from the riverbank. *A glance back here gives an excellent view of the Coldwell Rocks, home to Ravens and Peregrine Falcons. The latter are a visitor attraction, the RSPB providing telescopes to view the nest site from Yat Rock, during the summer months. These dramatically situated meadows have been used for a number of TV and film productions.*

After several hundred yards, the route goes over a stile and a short distance into woodland. Then the path turns and enters fields, **15** continuing along the riverbank. At the end of the fields cross the stile into the grounds adjacent to the factory, continue along to the bridge and cross over the river.

At the end of the bridge there is the entrance to another railway tunnel and a WWII pill box. Turn right here along the river bank.

Shortly the path passes Welsh Bicknor Youth Hostel, **16** a former Victorian rectory, and the adjacent St Margaret's church. The footpath then continues along the riverbank through several fields. *Midway around the bend in the river Courtfield can be seen on top of the rise to the left. The infant Henry V was nursed here, but what remains today is a rest-home for catholic missionaries.*

Continue along the river bank passing through Thomas Wood. The path at one stage is below and parallel to the former railway which emerged from the tunnel in Thomas Wood and crossed the river by a bridge. Only the abutment remains, adjoining the path.

Views of Goodrich Castle appear on the skyline directly in front of you as the path continues along the river bank.

Young Peregrine Falcons

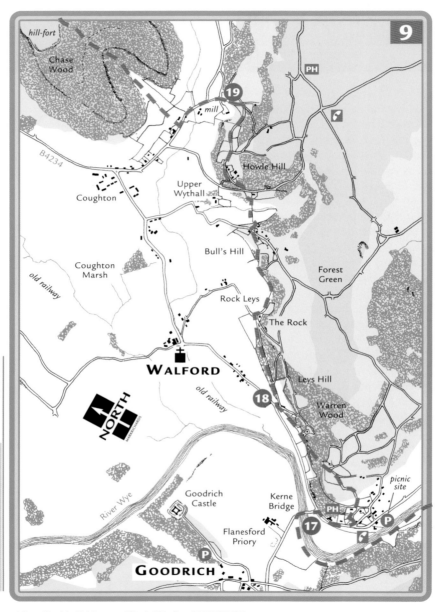

hill-fort

Chase
Wood

PH

19

mill

B4234

Howle Hill

Upper
Wythall

Coughton

Bull's Hill

Coughton
Marsh

Forest
Green

old railway

Rock Leys

The Rock

✠
WALFORD

Leys Hill

old railway

18

Warren
Wood

NORTH
MAPANDGRAPHICS

picnic
site

River Wye

Goodrich
Castle

Kerne
Bridge

PH

P

17

Flanesford
Priory

P

GOODRICH

ONE MILE

ONE KILOMETRE

THOMAS WOOD TO CHASE WOOD

The path emerges into fields as you approach Kerne Bridge. Climb the steps up to the bridge, taking care on this busy corner, and cross over the river. **17** *A glance back here again reveals Goodrich Castle against the skyline. This is an impressive Norman fortification, managed by English Heritage and open daily throughout the year.*

At the T junction turn right along a path parallel to the B4234 road. After passing the former Kerne Bridge Railway Station and the new Bishopswood Village Hall, go left to reach a bus shelter. The route crosses the road here, however, if you continue for a few yards you will come to a riverside parking and picnic area.

Walk up the lane opposite for around 15 yards, then turn left and go up the first driveway. To the rear of Falcon House take the steps on your right, and go up the next drive.

At the next junction of drives continue straight on uphill. Some of the surroundings, such as wall and trees, suggest this may once have been a bridleway or track, though it is only registered as a footpath now. At the

Goodrich Castle

Canoeists at Kerne Bridge and Picnic Site

end of the path turn left and continue between two houses.

At this point the main route continues off to the left. Bearing right here will take you on a 2 mile loop walk through beech woods and back along the Wye Valley Walk to your start point.

Following the main route, head downhill through beech woods, shady in summer, and past an old quarry site, soon meeting a lane, partially surfaced in concrete. Keep to the left going downhill for several hundred yards passing Cherry Tree Cottage on the right. The concrete surface is treacherous in wet conditions. Just

before meeting the road **18** turn right and head back uphill, following a concrete drive. The woodland here was coppiced, (felled and allowed to regrow from the stumps), a few years ago. Bluebells flourish here in the Spring.

Just before reaching a cottage the loop walk rejoins the main route (by the path coming in from the right). Ignore the tarmac drive leading down from the cottage and take a narrow track downhill, parallel to and veering away from, the drive. Continue straight on inside the edge of the wood. The next road you meet ascends Bulls Hill. Cross it and go through the entrance to the house, then go left around the building and through the garden to the field below.

Bear left to the bottom corner of the field. The stream here runs even in the driest summers. Climb up the field, and cross the stile. The path shortly leads to the road on Howle Hill. Cross it and proceed along the bridleway ahead. Ignore steps going downhill opposite the first house on the right. Carry on up the lane past another house on the right. Follow the track around to the right, then at Still Meadow House which is on the left of the route, turn left.

At the next cottage leave the track by turning left over the stile into a meadow. *There are some prominent ant hills developing here. This is a sign of a well established and undisturbed grassland. an increasingly rare and important habitat.*

At the other side of the meadow head right under some fine old oak and beech. After several stiles you emerge on to the road at Coughton. **19** Turn left here and then right through the first farmyard, taking a stile by the left-hand gate. Continue through the next two gates and up the edge of the field to the wood. You are starting the climb on to Chase Hill here. Follow the path up through the wood. Turn right on meeting the next track. You soon emerge on top of the hill.

Near Kerne Bridge

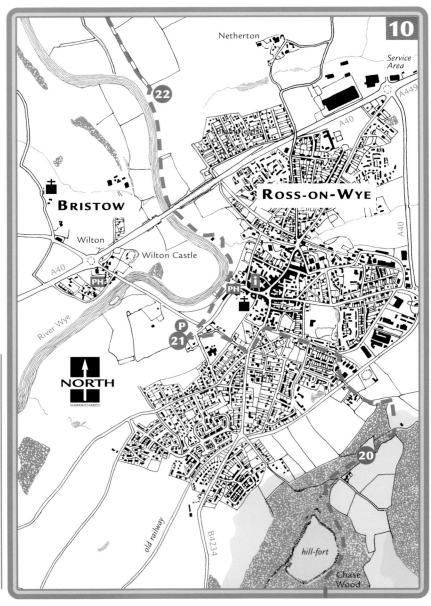

Netherton

Service Area

A449

A40

10

BRISTOW

ROSS-ON-WYE

Wilton

A40

Wilton Castle

A40

PH

PH

i

River Wye

P
21

NORTH
MARKRICHARDS

ONE MILE

ONE KILOMETRE

old railway

B4234

20

hill-fort

Chase Wood

22

CHASE WOOD TO ROSS-ON-WYE AND BEYOND

Here forestry tracks meet around a large Redwood tree. *The top of the hill is the site of an Iron Age fort which once covered more than 20 acres.* Follow the track straight ahead and down to Hill Farm. You enter Merrivale wood here directly in front of you. It is managed as a nature reserve by the Herefordshire Nature Trust.

At the end of the wood by a new memorial seat, **20** climb the stile and carry on in the same direction. At the next oak turn left and follow the track around to the right over a further two stiles into Tank meadow, so named after the 19th century reservoir at the top, which supplies the town of Ross below.

Stay on the left of the field and at the bottom turn left through an obscured kissing gate. *The timber framed building reached shortly is Alton Court, now the headquarters of PGL adventure holidays.*

Wye in flood

Just before a right hand bend the route goes off to the left through a gap in some fence panels. This leads to Blake Avenue. Follow this quiet cul-de-sac around to the right to its junction with Merrivale Lane, then turn right and after a few yards left, and cross the road. Entering a narrow footpath here, carry on straight ahead through two metal kissing gates, to the main road. If you wish to visit the market town of Ross, turn right here.

Ross-on-Wye sits attractively on a rise above the river, with a backdrop of wooded hills. The market house situated in the middle of the town is still the focus of a small market on Thursdays and Saturdays and there are good views over the river from the Prospect Gardens, behind St Mary's Church. There is a cattle market at Overross.

Cross the main road and continue straight ahead to the end of a private road, where you go left through another metal kissing gate. *The John Kyrle walk, a 2 mile circular walk, leaves the main route here.* To follow the main route continue to the bottom of the steps, turn right and then bear left at a five way fingerpost. Carry on down a further flight of steps to Wilton Car Park. **21** Once over the footbridge turn right and go through an archway beneath the road.

Bear slightly left and head towards a white building. 'The Riverside Restaurant'. Cross the road just before it and follow the riverbank. *Upstream, The Hope and Anchor has a pleasant riverside garden here, and there are short boat trips run from the launch point.* Follow the riverbank a little further and then cut across the green towards the Rowing club entrance.

On reaching Ross rowing club, cross over the small concrete footbridge. Turn left and follow the fence line around to a second concrete footbridge. Cross this and bear right to follow the riverbank upstream. *However, first of all pause and look back at the excellent views of Ross overlooking the Wye.*

Passing beneath the A40 road bridge, continue to follow the riverbank until the field narrows. Cross the narrow neck of the field to your right, then go left onto a disused railway line. **22** *This was one of the first lines to be closed under the Beeching cuts. The last trains ran in 1964. The line is waymarked as a permissive route (by permission of the landowner*

Fly Agaric

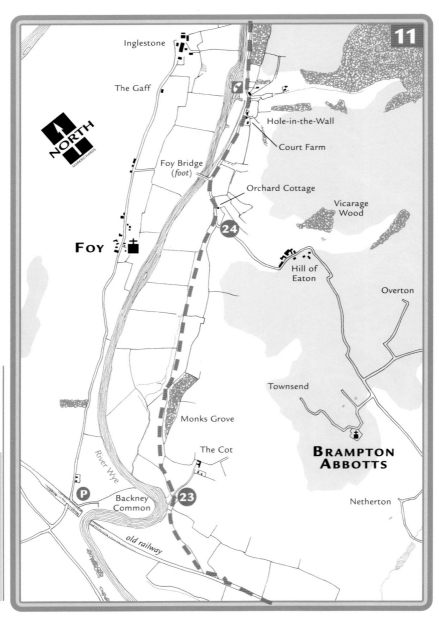

Inglestone

The Gaff

NORTH
MARKRICHARDS

Foy Bridge
(foot)

FOY

Hole-in-the-Wall

Court Farm

Orchard Cottage

Vicarage
Wood

24

Hill of
Eaton

Overton

Townsend

Monks Grove

The Cot

**BRAMPTON
ABBOTTS**

River Wye

ONE MILE

ONE KILOMETRE

P
Backney
Common

23

Netherton

old railway

11

BEYOND ROSS-ON-WYE TO HOLE-IN-THE-WALL

After encountering several large blocks of stone and crossing a farm track, continue for a further 150 yards, then turn right down some steps and follow the eastern edge of the field directly in front until you come out by the river again. Turn right on to the track. *If you look left here, you will see the piers of what was Backney rail bridge.*

Turn left across a small stream at the next gate opening and follow the hedge line ahead. **23** Where the hedge straggles to an end, bear right to join the corner of a wood. This is Monks Grove, replanted with help from the Countryside Service during the 1980s. Go straight past the first stile and follow the field edge with the wood on your right: it is colourful with flowers during the spring months. At the end of the field turn right into the end of the wood for a short distance, before entering another field again. Follow the hedge ahead of you. The 3 trees on your right are Hornbeams, an unusual tree in Herefordshire.

About two-thirds of the way along the second field bear slightly right towards a large oak tree with a gate at its base ahead of you at the end of the field. Go through the gate and proceed between the hedge and the conifer plantation. *The church on your left is Foy. Most of what you see is 14th Century but the original structure dates to 1050 and was dedicated to St Ffwy. As the Normans refused to recognise Celtic saints, they turned this into Saint Faith, (Foi in French), and later into Saint Mary. There may be mute swans grazing in the riparian fields, also Canada Geese and buzzards hovering overhead.*

24 When you reach the road turn left and you will see the graceful span of Foy footbridge ahead. Follow the road past the bridge. Court Farm on your right is now an activity centre. Carry on through the hamlet of Hole in the Wall and over a cattle grid.

Foy church

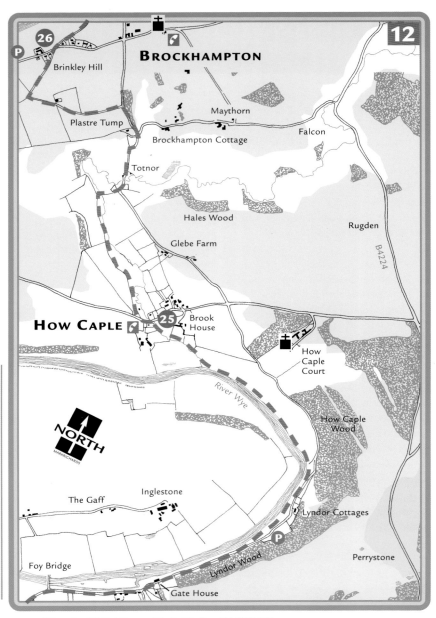

BROCKHAMPTON

26

P

Brinkley Hill

Plastre Tump

Maythorn

Brockhampton Cottage

Falcon

Totnor

Hales Wood

Rugden

Glebe Farm

B4224

HOW CAPLE

25

Brook House

How Caple Court

River Wye

How Caple Wood

NORTH

MARKRICHARDS

Inglestone

The Gaff

Lyndor Cottages

Foy Bridge

Perrystone

Lyndor Wood

P

Gate House

ONE MILE

ONE KILOMETRE

12

HOLE-IN-THE-WALL TO BROCKHAMPTON

Continue along the road until reaching the second cattle grid, then head off left to the riverbank and cross the footbridge. Follow the river bank until you reach a stream at the end of the field. Then bear right continuing to walk along the field edge with the stream on your left until you emerge on the road at How Caple. **25** Turn left here and then right beyond the phone box, to follow a bridleway past some stables and "The Old Mill House".

Go through a gate and continue along the track into a field. Then follow the curving field edge in front of you.

Nearing the end of the narrow field, turn right to cross a further footbridge, and go straight up to the right-hand side of the cottage. At the road turn left and drop down through the hamlet of Totnor. The redbrick building on your left after crossing the stream used to be a Blacksmiths forge. Keep following the road uphill then turn left at the waymarked third trackway on your left.

While you are recovering your breath, admire the view from the field gate back to *Ross, with St Mary's Spire showing against Chase Hill.*

At the end of the track turn right and head up the field edge towards the white houses. On reaching the road go straight across and follow the track besides Luiten House, **26** the old stone school building with its bell. This is a part of the scattered community of Brockhampton.

Otter

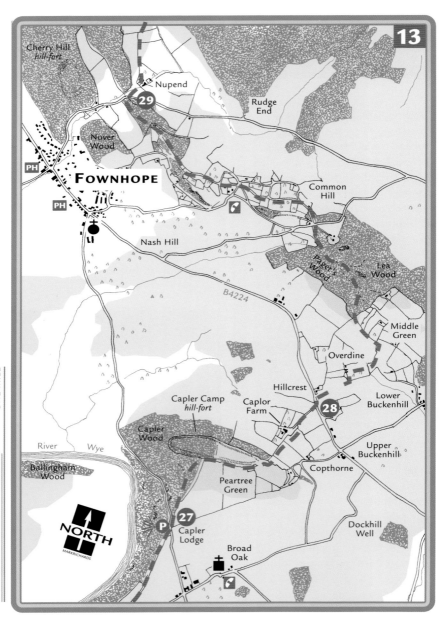

ONE MILE

ONE KILOMETRE

13

Cherry Hill
hill-fort

Nupend

29

Rudge
End

Nover
Wood

PH

FOWNHOPE

PH

Common
Hill

Nash Hill

Pager's
Wood

Lea
Wood

B4224

Middle
Green

Overdine

Hillcrest

Capler Camp
hill-fort

Caplor
Farm

Lower
Buckenhill

28

Capler
Wood

River   Wye

Upper
Buckenhill

Ballingham
Wood

Copthorne

NORTH
MARKRICHARDS

Peartree
Green

27
P

Capler
Lodge

Dockhill
Well

Broad
Oak

O n reaching the next road turn left. This is almost the top of Capler Hill with its picnic site, viewpoint and small car park. **27**

Just beyond the cottage bear right up a track.

Bear right on reaching a conifer plantation and shortly enter a field where you walk between the defences of yet another Iron Age Fort. *There is no evidence that this was ever occupied and it may have been constructed as a fortress retreat in times of need.*

100 yards after passing the barn, bear left off the track and negotiate a flight of steps down a steeply wooded bank. Follow the edge of two fields, skirting around a new bungalow and cross over a stile on your left into the driveway of Caplor Farm. Turn right up to the road and then left. Cross over and take the first driveway on the right. **28**

Walk up the track and at the first bend go over a stile on your right adjacent to a gate. Traverse the field to a stile in the boundary hedge facing you. Cross the stile and continue to follow the

Wye from Capler viewpoint

edge of the field on your right. Once through the metal gate at the bottom of the field, follow the next hedge keeping it on your left to a stile at the top of the field. Then bear left. After a further four fields you enter Pagetts Wood, a Herefordshire Nature Trust reserve. Watch out for Fallow Deer here.

At the next junction of paths turn left. Just before you leave the wood a pair of lime kilns can be seen on your right. Follow the fence up to the road, cross over and continue up the driveway opposite. Take the left fork and at the top of the slope turn right over a stile, and then left along the ridge path.

The many depressions and hollows alongside the path are disused limestone quarries. After a short distance you pass a seat with a good view of the Wye Valley and drop down through a meadow. *This is another small nature reserve, rich in wildflowers and butterflies during the summer months. The black and white 'Marbled White' butterfly, is of particular interest because it is uncommon in the County.*

Follow the path down to a crossroads of paths and tracks.

At the cross roads continue straight ahead, that is uphill. Shortly, as you emerge out into the open, there is a good view of the west side of Haugh

wood, (across to the right). This is one of the largest blocks of woodland in the county.

The ridge top is soon reached. *This is Common Hill, one of several limestone ridges that make up the Woolhope hills. Some interesting limestone flora can be seen during spring and summer, including a few species of orchid.* The village of Fownhope and the River Wye can also be glimpsed through the trees off to the left here.

Where a path drops off to your left continue straight on, staying on the high ground, and then go down hill past the next cottage. On reaching the road cross over and go down the track opposite. **29** However, if you wish to visit the village of Fownhope, turn left down this road. *The attractive village centre is reached in ½ a mile. Amenities include shops, a post office and three inns. There is an attractive Norman church, and the village remains one of the few to celebrate oak apple day each May.*

After leaving the road again, the route descends the trackway for a few yards, then turn right, and after a few more yards go left through the right hand one of three gates marked as a bridleway. Continue along the edge of the fence and then straight across the open field to another stile. Follow the left-hand side of the hedge opposite you.

Fownhope and orchards

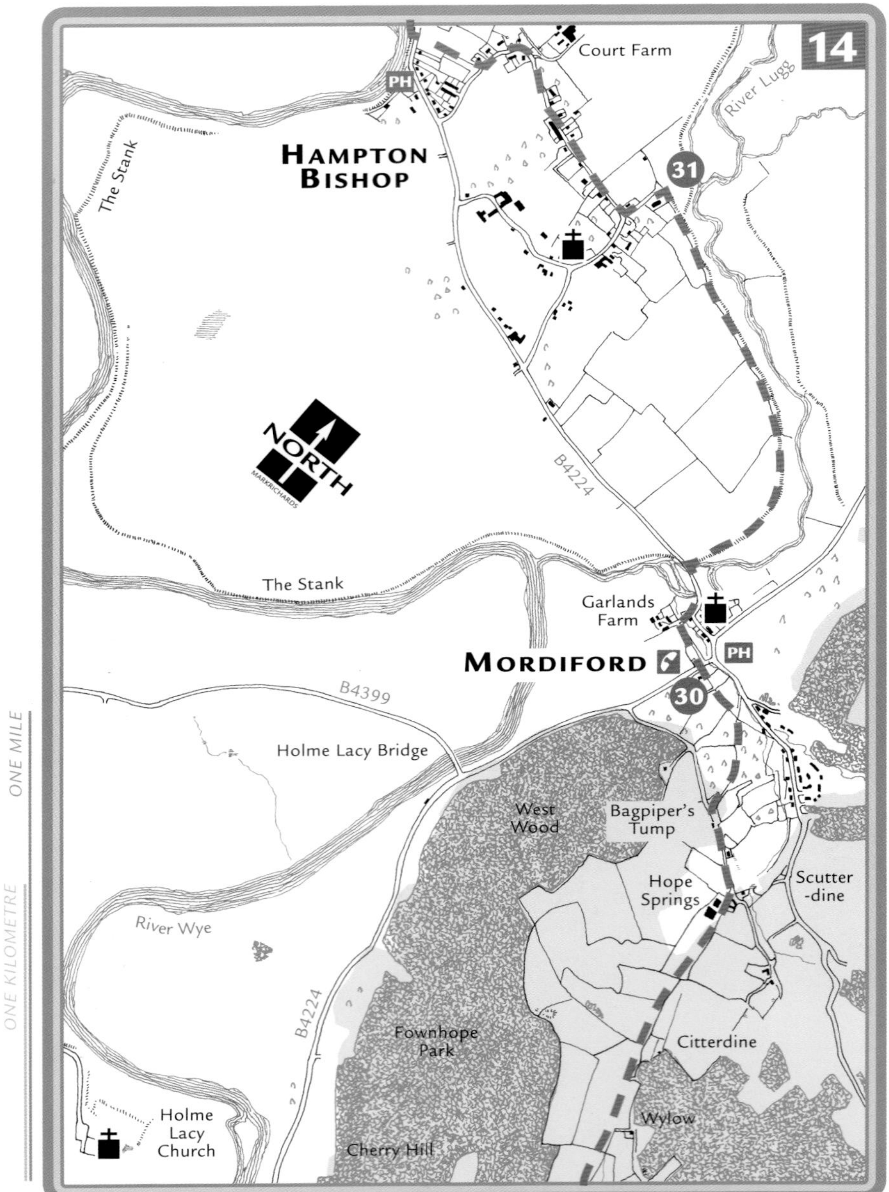
14
Court Farm
PH
River Lugg
HAMPTON BISHOP
31
The Stank
NORTH
MARKRICHARDS
B4224
The Stank
Garlands Farm
MORDIFORD
PH
30
B4399
Holme Lacy Bridge
West Wood
Bagpiper's Tump
Hope Springs
Scutter -dine
River Wye
B4224
Fownhope Park
Citterdine
Holme Lacy Church
Wylow
Cherry Hill
ONE MILE
ONE KILOMETRE

Once through the next gate, follow a well defined track towards a large field Oak. The Wye Valley Walk continues through a gate at the end of this field, and straight on down the driveway ahead. Pass through the farmyard and after a few yards turn left along the road. A little way along there are remnants of some lovely old orchards, bedecked with mistletoe.

You will pass two cottages on the right. After 100 yards take the driveway to the right, and the footpath to the right after a few yards. After entering the orchard bear left and follow the hedgerow. Cross over the stile and continue along to the farm buildings. Bear right around these. As you enter the farmyard there is a mill on the left with an intact wheel. **30**

Orchards near Mordiford

You are entering the village of Mordiford here, with the Moon Inn on your right.

There is an optional loop walk from the village. This is around four miles in length and takes you deeper into the Woolhope Hills. Free leaflets of this loop walk are available from the village pub and shop. The village grew up at an ancient ford over the River Lugg, though this is now crossed by a nine arched bridge constructed in the 16th century. Local folklore tells of a fearsome dragon that terrorised the village and was eventually slain by a condemned man promised his freedom in return for the deed.

Cross over the road and continue along the trackway, turning right at the next T junction. This crosses the Pentaloe Brook and leads shortly to the post office and store.

Turn left along the road and cross the bridge. This river is the Lugg, which joins the river Wye just a few hundred yards down stream.
At the end of the bridge turn right over the stile and double back on yourself up onto the flood bank. Pause and look back at the attractive view of Mordiford, with its church of Norman origin and the former rectory. Turn left and continue along the bank for approximately ³/₄ mile, passing through several gates. *Sufton, the home of the Hereford family, Lords of the manor since the 12th Century, stands prominently off to the right.*

When you reach a stock-holding pen, turn left along the lane, **31** and then right at the next junction. *This is the village of Hampton Bishop. If you wish to visit the interesting picturesque Norman Church of St Andrew with its unusual ground plan and mediaeval roof timbers, go left.* Otherwise follow Rectory Road to the right for about half a mile. Keep going until you reach a finger post next to a 4 ft brick garden wall. Leave the road to the right. Enter the field and head straight across to a stile on the edge of the road. The route goes straight on here, however, if refreshments are required, the Bunch of Carrots public house lies 150 yards down the road to the left.

Hereford cattle

Mordiford

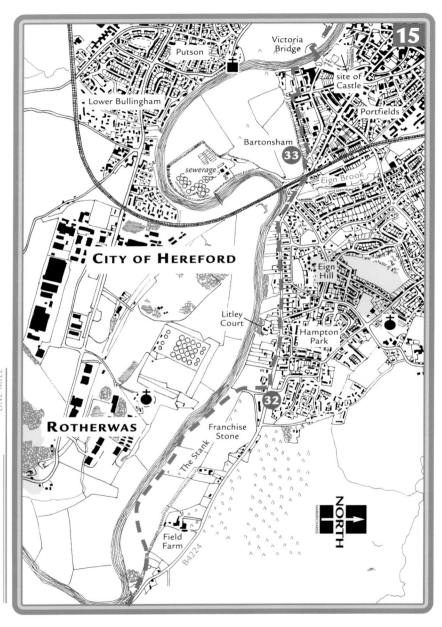

ONE MILE

ONE KILOMETRE

15

Victoria Bridge

Putson

site of Castle

Lower Bullingham

Portfields

Bartonsham **33**

sewerage

Eign Brook

CITY OF HEREFORD

Eign Hill

Litley Court

Hampton Park

ROTHERWAS

32

Franchise Stone

The Stank

NORTH

Field Farm

B4224

HAMPTON BISHOP TO HEREFORD (VICTORIA BRIDGE)

Cross over the road here and up the steps onto the flood bank. Turn immediately right through a kissing gate and continue along the flood bank. Just beyond the next kissing gate veer off left down to the footbridge and from here across the field to the riverbank. Turn right through a kissing gate and follow the riverbank for several fields. The hill on the opposite bank is Dinedor, one of a number in the area to be capped with Iron Age forts.

Eventually the route leads away from the river to a further kissing gate, situated in the corner of the field. Turn right from here. Pass a new housing estate on your left and go through three more kissing gates to meet the road into Hereford. **32** Cross over the road and turn left continuing along the road.

After you pass beneath a railway bridge, take the next left into Park Street. **33** At the end of this road turn right and first left into Vicarage Road. At the end pass down the pathway ahead to the river. Turn right along the riverbank up to the Victoria suspension bridge and cross the river into Bishops Meadow.

Church Street, Hereford

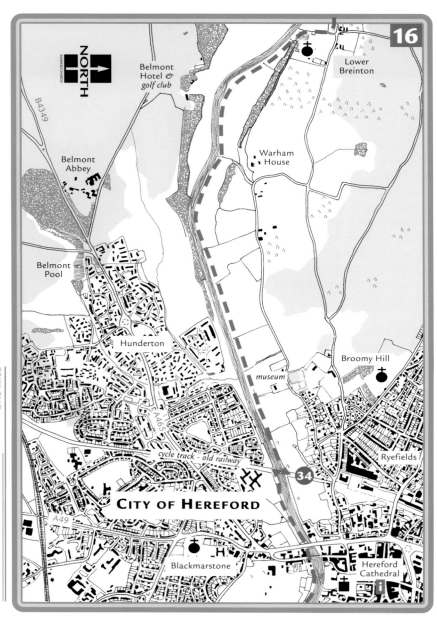

NORTH

16

Belmont Hotel & golf club

B4349

Lower Breinton

Belmont Abbey

Warham House

Belmont Pool

Hunderton

Broomy Hill

museum

A465

Ryefields

cycle track - old railway

34

ONE MILE

CITY OF HEREFORD

A49

ONE KILOMETRE

Blackmarstone

Hereford Cathedral

Turn right and follow the riverbank, with its view of the Cathedral, up to the old six arched Wye bridge.

The city grew up around an ancient river crossing, which explains its name, which means Ford of the army. Sites of interest include the Cathedral and Mappa Mundi, a 13th Century world map, now housed in a purpose built building along with a medieval chained library. Bulmers the cider makers are based here, and a cider museum is open to the public. There is a Waterworks Museum which is just off the Wye Valley Walk at Broomy Hill, based on a Victorian water pumping station. Also the well established Three Choirs Festival rotates annually between Hereford and the cities of Worcester and Gloucester.

Cross over the road on reaching the 15th Century Wye Bridge, remaining on the same side of the river. Shortly you pass under the new road bridge. Continue on to the disused railway bridge at Hunderton. Climb the steps to the left and cross over the bridge descending on to the opposite bank. **34** Continue along the riverbank. From here to Breinton is a popular riverside stroll from the city.

Despite its proximity to the city, the high pitched call and electric blue flash of the kingfisher are still occasionally encountered along this stretch.

The path soon emerges into open countryside again, and follows the riverbank through several fields with Belmont golf course on the opposite bank.

Where the footpath meets a wooded bank, the route ascends the slope. In the Spring there is a lovely display of flowers here. *At the top of the bank are earthworks which are thought to be the remains of a medieval moated manor house built during the 12th century. Behind this lies Breinton Church.*

Leave the car park by the vehicle track. The old orchard on the right is a mass of blossom in the spring.

Half way along this track go left through a metal kissing gate into a younger orchard. *There are a couple of trees here with good mistletoe growths. This unusual parasitic plant celebrated in folklore is now quite rare nationally, but is still common in Herefordshire.*

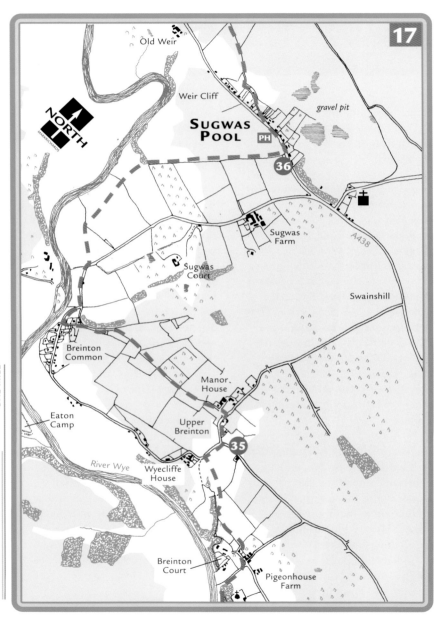

17

Old Weir

Weir Cliff

SUGWAS POOL PH

gravel pit

NORTH

36

Sugwas Farm

Sugwas Court

A438

Swainshill

Breinton Common

Manor House

Eaton Camp

Upper Breinton

35

River Wye

Wyecliffe House

Breinton Court

Pigeonhouse Farm

ONE MILE

ONE KILOMETRE

BREINTON CHURCH TO SUGWAS POOL

Cross the orchard diagonally and continue up the side of a house advertising B & B. Turn left into an arable field, keeping to the left hand side, and go on through a further field.

On reaching the road turn right, then left at the next road junction. **35** Just beyond the cottage turn left and follow the bridle path. Although the top of the hill is only 350 feet high, it does afford good views back into Hereford City and forward to the Welsh hills, giving an idea of the delights to come.

On reaching the top of the hill go through the right hand gate and

Primrose

follow the hedge around to the left through the bridle gate and down the track between houses to the road. There is a view of the river on the way. Turn right to descend the escarpment. On the right is a cottage with memorials carved into the beams.

At the bottom of the slope you can glimpse the river between the trees in winter. To the right of the road there are some fine old oaks and a gorse covered slope that appears to be home to a pair of buzzards.

At the next bend to the right go left over an old Sussex style fence and continue straight ahead to the corner of the hedge opposite. There is a double stile, (just to the left of the corner) climb it and head off in a direction about 11 o'clock to this. Head to the right of the tree with a dead top. As you clear the rise you should see the next stile in the hedge ahead of you. From here head for the gateway with adjacent stile in the next field, between a wood and orchard.

Once over the stile keep to the right hand edge of the next two fields until you reach the main road. **36** Cross the road here and turn left towards the Kites Nest Inn. Kites remain a very scarce sight over Herefordshire, though attempts to reintroduce this magnificent bird into parts of England are meeting with some success. So in time who knows?

At the end of the pavement bear right down a metalled road which develops into a wide lane between houses. Skirt around to the right of the last house and enter the field.

Sand Martin feeding young

Breinton Church

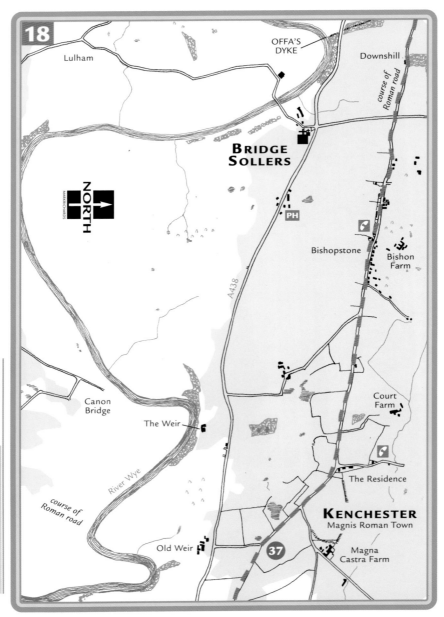

18

Lulham

OFFA'S
DYKE

Downshill

course of Roman road

BRIDGE SOLLERS

NORTH

MARK RICHARDS

PH

Bishopstone

Bishon Farm

A438

Canon Bridge

The Weir

Court Farm

River Wye

The Residence

course of Roman road

Old Weir

37

KENCHESTER
Magnis Roman Town

Magna Castra Farm

ONE MILE

ONE KILOMETRE

18

SUGWAS POOL TO GARNONS HILL

From here follow the hedge line straight ahead until you reach the road. At the road turn right. **37**

This is an old Roman road which shortly passes the site of the Roman walled town of Magnis. Sadly little is visible on the ground today.

After rejoining the road continue on past the Credenhill turn and a little further on the turn to Kenchester Church. Remaining on the main road here you pass through the village of Bishopstone, this eventually brings you to a crossroads, cross over following the sign to Garnons.

Apple Blossom

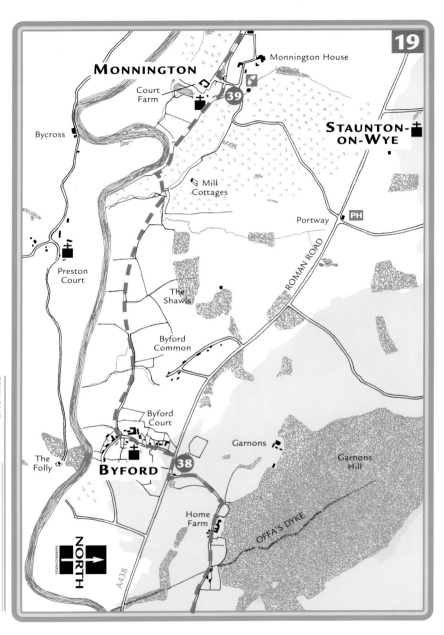

19

MONNINGTON

Monnington House

Court Farm

39

STAUNTON-ON-WYE

Bycross

Mill Cottages

Portway

PH

ROMAN ROAD

Preston Court

The Shawls

Byford Common

Byford Court

Garnons

Garnons Hill

The Folly

BYFORD

38

Home Farm

OFFA'S DYKE

NORTH

MARKRICHARDS

A438

ONE MILE

ONE KILOMETRE

GARNONS HILL TO MONNINGTON

On a clear day there are some fine views across towards the Black Mountains from this road. Soon some impressive parkland trees start to appear as you enter the Garnons Estate, home of the Cotterell family. Turn left at the end of the road and right on to the main road at the Gate House. **38** Caution is needed here, as this is a busy section of road.

Take the first road left signed to Byford. A 100 yards or so past the church, the route follows the bridleway off to the right.

On leaving the tarmac lane, keep following the wide track, which is a bridleway. On your right you will see some old fruit trees. The bridleway is well defined along the headland and has some fine large oaks.

At the far end of a group of poplars, the track takes a dog leg, right then left, with the next hedge on your right. At this point you will see a church and farm buildings on the left. These are Preston Court, which is in fact on the other side of the river.

Keep to the side of the field and cross over a stream in an orchard. Here you will find a Bulmers' notice board,

welcoming walkers and explaining their planting.

At the riverbank turn right and follow the edge of the orchard until you reach a small church on the left. This is St Mary's at Monnington. *Folklore suggests that Owain Glyndwr, the Welsh leader, was buried here in the 15th century.*

Go left into the churchyard and immediately right to a fine old Lych gate. Follow the path ahead with the steam on your right. When you reach the metalled driveway go left, **39** then curve right around the front of the red brick house to enter Monnington Walk, a wide avenue of varied Pine and Yew trees.

Hereford cattle

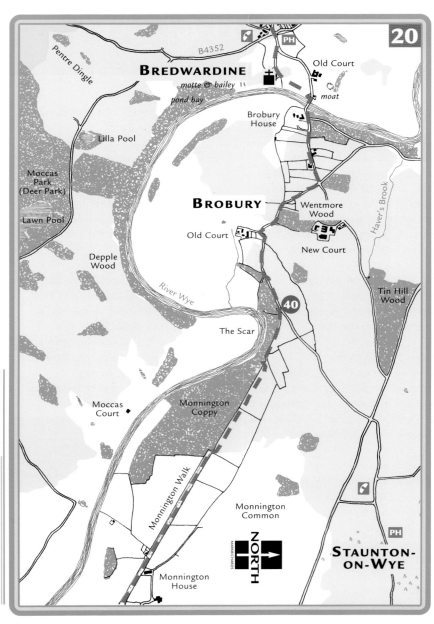

20

BREDWARDINE

B4352

Old Court

motte & bailey
pond bay

moat

Pentre Dingle

Brobury
House

Lilla Pool

Moccas
Park
(Deer Park)

BROBURY

Wentmore
Wood

Lawn Pool

Old Court

New Court

Depple
Wood

Haver's Brook

River Wye

Tin Hill
Wood

40

The Scar

Moccas
Court

Monnington
Coppy

Monnington
Walk

Monnington
Common

Monnington
House

NORTH

PH

**STAUNTON-
ON-WYE**

PH

ONE MILE

ONE KILOMETRE

MONNINGTON TO BREDWARDINE

Carry on to the end of the avenue. Then bear right through a gate and immediately left to follow the side of the wood. At the end of the second field go left through the bridle gate to re-enter the wood.

You are at the beginning of Brobury Scar here, where the river has cut deep into the sandstone to create a cliff-like bluff. Notice the gnarled old chestnut trees alongside the path too. Continue along the main path at the edge of the wood but take time to view the 300 foot drop to the river below, and across to Moccas Park in the distance. The Park was landscaped by Capability Brown.

On meeting the road turn left. **40** The large hill ahead is Merbach. The walk takes you over its summit. On reaching the no-through-road signs keep following the lane to the right. When the crossroads are reached turn left and follow the road down to Bredwardine bridge. Take care crossing the bridge then take the stile on the left. Go over the footbridge and bear slightly right to head for the church, where the writer Kilvert was vicar in the 1870s.

From the church continue down the drive along the avenue of beeches. Turn left at the road junction.

Brobury Scar

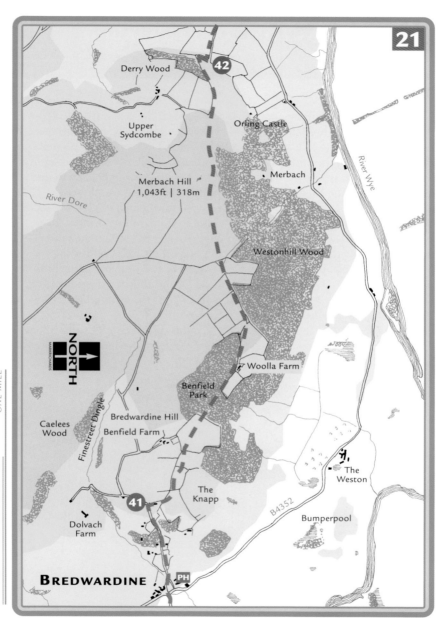

21

Derry Wood

42

Orling Castle

Upper
Sydcombe

Merbach

Merbach Hill
1,043ft | 318m

River Dore

Westonhill Wood

River Wye

NORTH

Woolla Farm

Benfield
Park

Caelees
Wood

Bredwardine Hill

Benfield Farm

The
Weston

41

The
Knapp

Dolvach
Farm

Bumperpool

B4352

BREDWARDINE

PH

ONE MILE

ONE KILOMETRE

At the crossroads, go straight over, taking the road just to the right of the Red Lion Hotel. At the top of a steep section of the hill turn right along the bridleway, just before cottages on the left. **41** Once through the farm gate follow the field edge around to the left. Pass through the next bridle gate and take a course 45° right across the field. Pass through the gap in the hedge and continue straight on until a farm track is reached. Turn right and follow this.

Just before reaching the farm, the path bears left up through the wood, re-emerging on to the track just beyond the farm. Continue up the hill with fine views over the flood plain below. At the crest of the hill pass through a gate, and then go on to a second gate alongside some farm buildings. Continue through a further three fields before finally reaching the open expanses of Merbach Common. Go right over the stile here and then xleft after 25 yards.

This is the haunt of buzzards and ravens, which can often be seen riding the up draught along the slopes. The route bears right just before the summit, *but a short detour to the left soon leads to the summit cairn at 1,043 feet. It is claimed that eleven counties may be seen from here on a clear day.*

The route starts to descend from here. **42** Nearing the bottom of the hill the path swings round to the right and shortly enters a sunken lane.

Wye from Merbach Hill

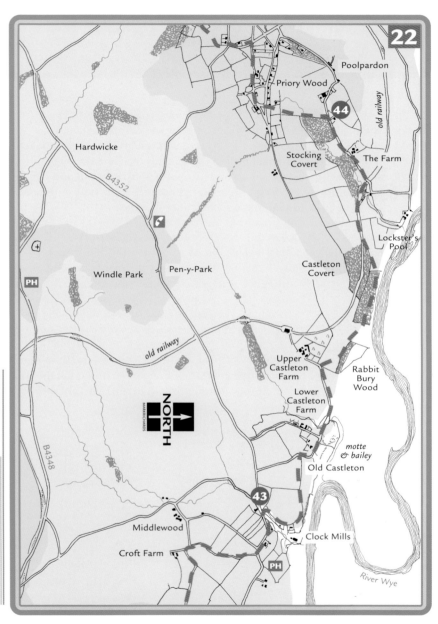

22

Poolpardon

Priory Wood

44

old railway

Hardwicke

B4352

Stocking
Covert

The Farm

Lockster's
Pool

Castleton
Covert

Windle Park

Pen-y-Park

PH

old railway

NORTH
MARRIE HARDS

Upper
Castleton
Farm

Rabbit
Bury
Wood

Lower
Castleton
Farm

motte
& bailey

Old Castleton

B4348

43

Middlewood

Clock Mills

Croft Farm

PH

River Wye

ONE MILE

ONE KILOMETRE

DERRY WOOD TO PRIORY WOOD

At the bottom of the lane bear left again and then right on reaching the metalled road signed to Middlewood. Leave the road again after a few yards and continue straight on along the track. The main road is reached next. Turn left here. However, if refreshments are required, the Castlefield Inn lies 100 yards up the road to the right.

Just past an impressive set of wrought iron gates, set back on the right, turn right on to a bridleway. **43** At the end of the grounds to the house turn left into the field and follow the field edge, emerging onto the road again opposite Old Castleton.

Turn right here and continue past Lower Castleton. Just before the top of the hill turn right through the gateway and head across the field, slightly down the slope, and go through an area of recently planted trees. Cross the bottom of the next field.

Wildfowl often gather on this stretch of river during the winter months. Wigeon, Teal and Goosander sometimes join the regular Mallard and Mute swans, and migratory Bewicks swan may occasionally be seen. Their musical trumpeting calls and yellow and black bills distinguish them from their resident cousins.

Pass through a short stretch of woodland then climb diagonally up the open slope ahead.

From the stile at the top there are good views over the meandering river towards Whitney Toll Bridge. The area below is known as Locksters Pool, one of several famous salmon pools along this stretch of river.

After a further field you enter another wood and follow the course of the disused Hereford to Brecon railway line. Just before you reach the bridge, turn left up through a gate and left along the road. Opposite Pool Pardon Cottage **44** turn left up into the field and continue through a further two fields to emerge on Clifford Common. Turn right and left, and then right again at the next T junction.

Follow the road until you reach a meadow which doubles as a football pitch and cut across to the left. Turn left again and follow the road down to a road junction.

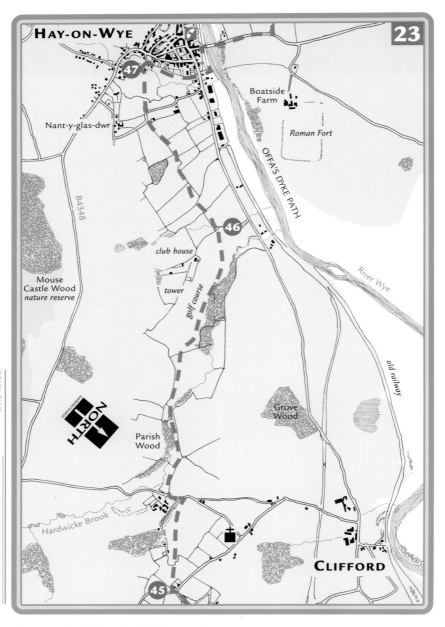

HAY-ON-WYE

23

47

Boatside
Farm

Roman Fort

Nant-y-glas-dwr

OFFA'S DYKE PATH

B4348

46

club house

River Wye

Mouse
Castle Wood
nature reserve

tower

golf course

NORTH

old railway

Grove
Wood

Parish
Wood

Hardwicke Brook

CLIFFORD

45

ONE MILE

ONE KILOMETRE

PRIORY WOOD TO HAY-ON-WYE

The route passes just to the left of the houses, goes straight across the first field and then over to the left to join a driveway down to the road. Turn left, and just past a large oak, right into the field. **45** The path follows an attractive dingle until you reach a ford and footbridge over Hardwicke Brook. Follow the right hand side of the hedge, veering off to the right just before the end of the field and cross the stile on to the golf course. Bear right at approximately 2 o'clock to the stile and follow the edge of the course. *The tower visible on the left is one of the few remaining features of 'The Moor'. The main house is now gone but a walled garden and fishponds remain, along with the avenue of trees ahead which is reached shortly.*

Just below the club house, head off left to a driveway and a stile. **46** Cross this to a further stile. Pass through a tree planted area and shortly you reach the avenue of trees, cross over, and head for a further stile in the corner of the field.

Hay-on-Wye with its castle is now clearly visible ahead. After a further three stiles the road is reached. Turn right and then on the next bend in the road take the footpath off to the left behind the bench. Drop down and over the dingle and once in the field head for the white gabled house opposite. Descend down to Dulas Brook, which marks the boundary with Wales and Powys.

47 Having crossed the Dulas Brook from Herefordshire take the path across Black Lion Green, with the cottages to the right, to the top of the bank where you enter Black Lion Lane. From here there is a choice, either, turn left into Hay itself, or turn right to stay on the Wye Valley Walk, which skirts the town.

Hay-on-Wye is well worth exploring. It is famous for its proliferation of second hand bookshops, and is the gateway to the next Welsh section of the Wye Valley.

Keeping to the walk, at the end of the lane go through the wicket gate and follow the enclosed path to Newport Street (B4350). Here, again, you can turn left along the road to explore Hay or keep on the Wye Valley Walk by taking Wyeford Road opposite to the riverside path. On reaching the river turn left along the riverbank path, walking below the cycle path. When the path passes below the road bridge over the River Wye turn left and zigzag up the ramp passing through the picnic area to the main road (B4351).

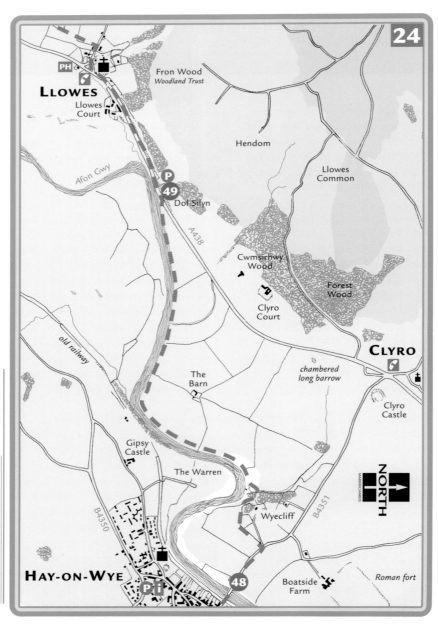

LLOWES

Fron Wood
Woodland Trust

Llowes
Court

Afon Gwy

P
49
Dol Silyn

A438

Hendom

Llowes
Common

Cwmsirhwy
Wood

Clyro
Court

Forest
Wood

old railway

The
Barn

*chambered
long barrow*

CLYRO

Clyro
Castle

Gipsy
Castle

The Warren

NORTH

B4351

Wyecliff

B4350

HAY-ON-WYE

P

48

Boatside
Farm

Roman fort

24

ONE MILE

ONE KILOMETRE

Leaving Hay, **48** cross the Wye Road Bridge and keep to the right hand footway. After 300 yards carefully cross the road to take the stile facing and follow the path along the edge of the field until you reach Wyecliff wood.

Once in Wyecliff Wood, turn right and with the high wall on your right continue downhill until the edge of the wood is reached. Leave the wood via a stile and footbridge and turn left. Follow the field edge passing a cottage on the left. The path now continues along the riverbank for 1½ miles, with large arable fields on your right. At the end of this riverside section head right over the field, pass over a stile and turn left.

49 A short path then leads to a lay-by at the edge of the main road (A438). Carefully cross the road, turn left and follow it for ½ mile until you reach the village of Llowes. This section of road is quite busy but the verges are wide and the visibility good.

Once at Llowes, turn right at the bus stop and telephone box opposite the Radnorshire Arms and follow the road through the village. After a short distance you reach a stile at the first field on the left. Cross this, and a second stile, then keep ahead ascending slightly to a stile that enters Bryn yr Hydd Common.

Hay-on-Wye bookshops

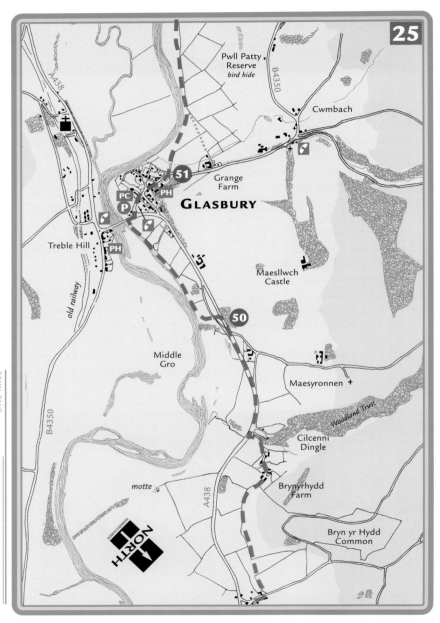

Pwll Patty
Reserve
bird hide

B4350

Cwmbach

Grange
Farm

51

PC

P

PH

GLASBURY

Treble Hill

PH

Maesllwch
Castle

old railway

50

Middle
Gro

Maesyronnen

Woodland Trust

Cilcenni
Dingle

B4350

motte

A438

Brynyrhydd
Farm

NORTH
MAXIMUM MAPS

Bryn yr Hydd
Common

25

ONE MILE

ONE KILOMETRE

BRYN YR HYDD COMMON TO GLASBURY FARM

Carry on climbing through sparse trees and bracken, following the track, faint at times, before meeting a bridleway coming in from the right. Veer left and pass through Brynyrhydd farmyard.

Continue down the lane until you meet the main road (A438). Cross over the road and turn right, keeping on the wide verge for about $^1/_2$ mile, passing the turn for Maesyronnen on the right.

50 Soon after this, turn left through a kissing gate, then cross the small field ahead and go through two more kissing gates into the next field. On entering this field, bear half right to where the path meets the river edge at another kissing gate.

Now follow the riverside path through several gates, passing a small water treatment works, until you emerge on to the main road at Glasbury Bridge. The fields here are dotted with fine oak trees and mistletoe can be seen hanging from a line of poplars bordering the river.

Carefully cross the road and go through the small car park with toilets. Bear left at the car park entrance and join the road through the village passing the Maesllwch Arms pub. A short distance beyond the pub the road bears right.

51 Take the track on the left leading into a field and continue ahead to the track at the far side near the river. Go through the gate and keep on the track past Glasbury Farm House.

Glasbury-on-Wye

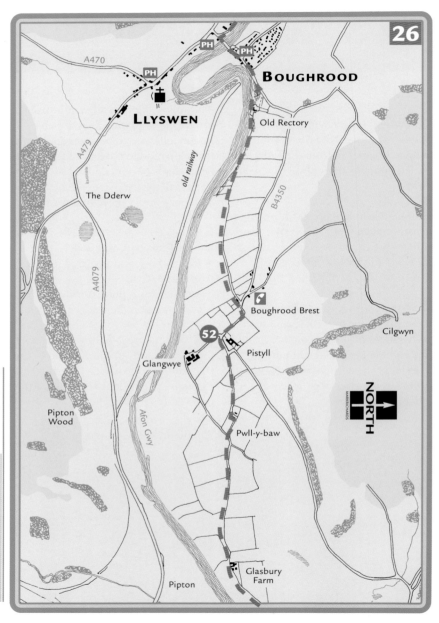

ONE MILE

ONE KILOMETRE

26

A470

PH

PH

PH

BOUGHROOD

LLYSWEN

Old Rectory

A479

old railway

B4350

The Dderw

A4079

Boughrood Brest

Cilgwyn

52

Pistyll

Glangwye

NORTH

MARIERCHARDS

Pipton
Wood

Afon Gwy

Pwll-y-baw

Pipton

Glasbury
Farm

Once through Glasbury Farm the old lane is lost for the next two fields as the hedge on the left has been removed, but beyond this the lane reappears. Where the lane bends left fork right through a gate that leads to Pwll-y-baw (which means mucky pool). Leave the ruins to your right and then keep ahead to the B4350 at Pistyll Farm.

52 Turn left and with care follow the road past Glangwy Farm entrance and onto Boughrood Brest. With telephone and post box ahead turn left on the track between cottages and continue to the open fields.

At the end of the second field enter the strip of woodland with the river below. Follow the path along until the gate of the Old Rectory is approached. If the river level is not high take the steps down to the waters edge and follow the path along the river and then up to the road. If the riverside path is flooded go through the gate and follow the right of way through the Old Rectory garden and grounds to the road. Turn left and Boughrood is a short distance ahead.

Kingfisher

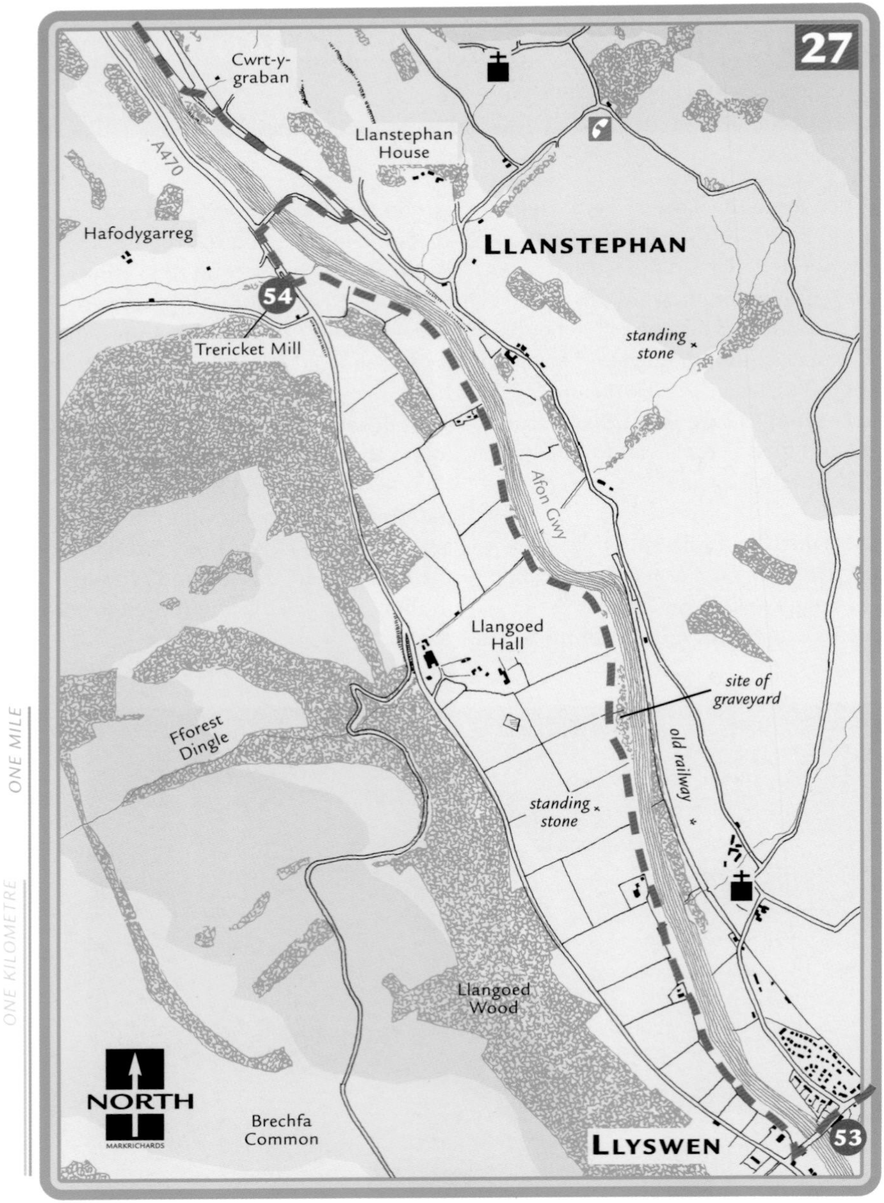
27
Cwrt-y-graban
Llanstephan House
A470
Hafodygarreg
LLANSTEPHAN
54
Trericket Mill
standing stone
Afon Gwy
Llangoed Hall
site of graveyard
old railway
Fforest Dingle
standing stone
Llangoed Wood
NORTH
MARKRICHARDS
Brechfa Common
LLYSWEN
53
ONE KILOMETRE
ONE MILE

Pass the Post Office and pub in Boughrood **53** and at the far side of the bridge turn right on the tarmaced riverside lane that you follow to the Water Treatment Works where it becomes an unsurfaced footpath.

The riverside path now continues for 1½ miles, via a number of stiles. Along this section you pass by the old Llangoed Estate graveyard, with Llangoed Hall away to the left.

Llangoed Hall is now a magnificent Country House Hotel, that was bought by Sir Bernard Ashley in 1987, who restored it to its former glory. The Hall was formerly known locally as Llangoed Castle and there appears to have been a house on the site since 560AD. It is said that the first Welsh Parliament was held here.

Further along, the path passes an old barn and goes past the branching track leading to Llangoed Farm. The path finally reaches the point where the Sgithwen Brook joins the Wye. Here turn left and follow the brook to the main road (A470).
54 Turn right along the road, passing Trericket Mill and after 250 yards turn right again, crossing the river over the wonderful Llanstephan suspension bridge, one of the very few wooden

decked suspension bridges left in Wales.

Continue along the road to where it crosses the old railway line, beyond which there is a T-junction, here turn left along the road.

Just past the bridge abutments, 600 yards along the road from the T-junction, turn left over a stile onto a track.

Llanstephan Bridge

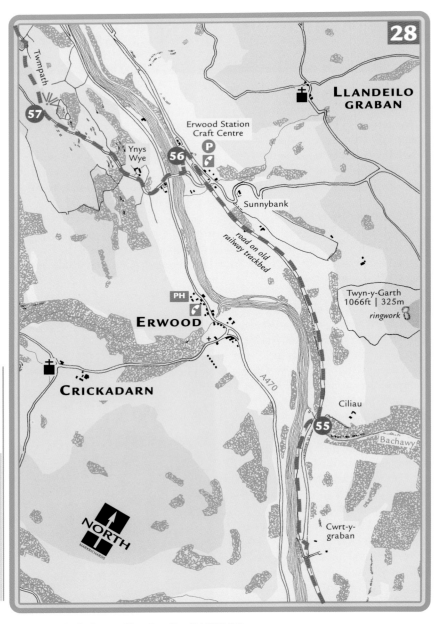

28

Twmpath

57

Ynys Wye

56

Erwood Station Craft Centre

P

Sunnybank

road on old railway trackbed

LLANDEILO GRABAN

Twyn-y-Garth
1066ft | 325m

ringwork

PH

ERWOOD

CRICKADARN

A470

Ciliau

55

Bachawy

NORTH
MARKRICHARDS

Cwrt-y-graban

ONE MILE

ONE KILOMETRE

LLANSTEPHAN TO TWMPATH

Bear right and follow the track along the riverside until you come to a small field where you follow the track right to a gate and the footbridge over the River Bachawy. Now join the track that passes under the old railway viaduct and at the top of the short rise go left over the stile to the road.

55 Turn right and follow the road bounded by a roadside nature reserve partly managed by Radnorshire Wildlife Trust. Follow the road for about a mile before reaching Erwood Old Station. As you approach the Old Station the road bears right, but carry straight on here across the picnic area and car park.

The Old Station is well worth a visit as it houses an interesting craft centre and refreshments are normally available.

56 The Wye Valley Walk leaves through a small metal gate at the edge of the picnic area. Follow the path that soon passes Bridge Cottage and leads on to the road.

Once on the road, turn right and cross over the bridge across the Wye to quickly join the junction with the main A470.

Crossing the A470, take the minor road opposite leading to Twmpath Common. The lane soon starts to climb steeply, passing an adjoining footpath on the left and Ynys-Wye farm on the right. Continue onward, crossing a cattle grid and onto the common.

Passing some small rock outcrops, after $^1/_4$ mile there is a wide stony track to the left and public rights of way to both left and right. This elevated position offers superb views of the Wye Valley.

Near Erwood

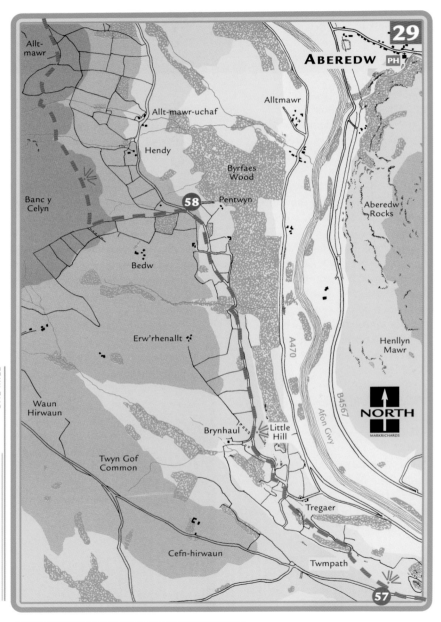

ALLT-MAWR

29

ABEREDW PH

Allt-mawr

Allt-mawr-uchaf

Alltmawr

Hendy

Byrfaes Wood

Banc y Celyn

58 Pentwyn

Aberedw Rocks

Bedw

Erw'rhenallt

Henllyn Mawr

Waun Hirwaun

A470

B4567

Afon Gwy

NORTH

MARKRICHARDS

Brynhaul

Little Hill

Twyn Gof Common

Tregaer

Cefn-hirwaun

Twmpath

57

ONE MILE

ONE KILOMETRE

Take the path on the right, **57** heading north west and leading down the partially bracken-covered slope across the open common. At the base of the slope a stile and fingerpost mark the point where you leave the common.

Beyond the stile an old trackway can clearly be seen, follow this until it starts to open out. Follow the signed path ahead leading to a gate and stile. Continue on the old lane ahead to a footbridge that crosses the Fernant stream and then leads up to a minor road.

Turn left at the road and follow it to the top of the hill and onto Little Hill Common, passing New House on the way. Where the road levels out at the top of the hill fine views of the valley may be gained, including Aberedw Rocks.

Ignore two bridleway signs to the left and continue along the road following the edge of the common. Keep on this metalled road for almost 1 mile until meeting the junction of the Old Bedw access track.

58 Turn left up this track and continue straight ahead up the bridleway leading to the common, ignoring the trackway leading to Old Bedw on the left. Once on the common keep to the path that follows the fence line uphill on the left for 500 yards, then turn right and follow the adjoining bridleway across the common.

Carry on over the open hill, crossing two small streams and passing a small pool, beyond which there is a field gate. The field ahead is the first of two that edge onto the hill, between which lies a small section of common. Upon entering the first of the two fields, follow the old hedge line ahead keeping to the left of it. This leads to a gate, pass through and cross the small section of common to the second field. Go through the gate and walk straight ahead keeping the fence line on the right. Further on an old wall appears to the right of the path with attractive ferns and other plants growing on it.

Looking towards Twmpath

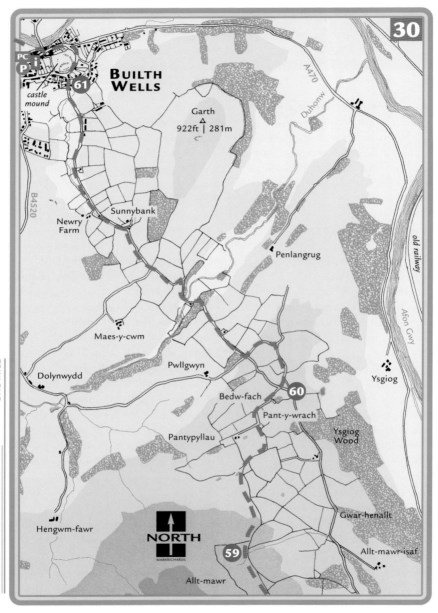

30

BUILTH WELLS

PC
P
61
castle mound

Garth
△
922ft | 281m

A470

Duhonw

old railway

Afon Gwy

Sunnybank

Newry Farm

Penlangrug

Maes-y-cwm

Pwllgwyn

Dolynwydd

Ysgiog

Bedw-fach
60

Pant-y-wrach

Pantypyllau

Ysgiog Wood

B4520

Hengwm-fawr

NORTH
MARKROCHARDS

59

Gwar-henallt

Allt-mawr-isaf

Allt-mawr

ONE MILE

ONE KILOMETRE

Continue along the fence line **59** until a gate is reached. Once through the gate, turn right and keeping the fence line on the right head down the hill until a gate is reached. Here you finally leave the open hill.

The path now follows a track which in places is edged with gorse and passes a junction with a footpath on the right. Keep to the track passing through two gates beyond which is a lane, with good views towards Builth Wells.

At this point the remnants of a small enclosure are marked on the map at Pant-y-Wrach, which translated means Witches Hollow, perhaps the site of a dwelling.

Pass through the gate, into the lane and turn right and follow the lane until it meets a minor road at Bedw Fach crossroads.

60 Cross straight over and follow the unsurfaced lane swinging left after 300 yards towards the next crossroads. Here, turn right down a sunken lane, passing Dolfach Cottage to the River Duhonw.

Walk over the footbridge crossing the river and follow the tarmac lane.

Go up this tarmac lane until it meets another lane (Newry Road). Keep to the right and continue to Builth Wells, passing a number of dwellings, including Newry Farm on the left, crossing the Gloe Brook at Tanhouse Bridge.

61 At the southern outskirts of Builth Wells, the Walk meets Castle Road. Here, turn right along Castle Road, leading onto Castle Street and into the town. The remains of the once important castle are now buried under grassy mounds.

Turn left along Castle Street to the next road junction, with the Wyeside Arts Centre on the right. Opposite there are two roads, on the left is Broad Street leading to the town centre, however take the road on the right, known as The Strand, which leads to The Groe - the town park and recreation area, with Tourist Information Centre.

During the Victorian era Builth Wells became a popular place to take the waters. It has now gained new importance by becoming the permanent headquarters of the Royal Welsh Show.

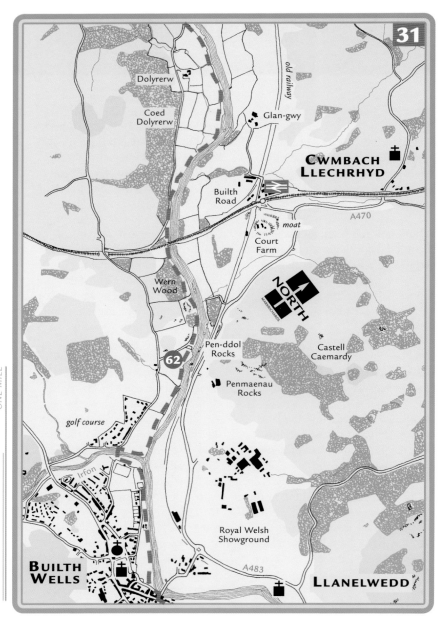

ONE MILE

ONE KILOMETRE

Dolyrerw

Coed
Dolyrerw

Glan-gwy

old railway

**CWMBACH
LLECHRHYD**

Builth
Road

Builth Road

A470

moat

Court
Farm

Wern
Wood

NORTH

Castell
Caemardy

62

Pen-ddol
Rocks

Penmaenau
Rocks

golf course

Irfon

Royal Welsh
Showground

A483

**BUILTH
WELLS**

LLANELWEDD

31

BUILTH WELLS TO DOLYRERW

On entering The Groe, the walk continues along a tree-lined avenue that follows the edge of the Wye to the confluence with the River Irfon, then along the River Irfon to the metal suspension bridge. Cross the bridge to the edge of a minor road, here turn right and pass through a kissing gate and along the other side of the River Irfon to meet back up with the Wye. The path now continues along the river edge through three fields towards Penddol Rocks.

The Walk now passes the impressive Penddol Rocks that form a mix of rapids and deep pools, particularly after heavy rain. Please note that it is dangerous to try to explore these rocks.

62 Leaving the field the path keeps close to the river, passes a small wooden bungalow, then carries on through some woods and plantations and under the railway bridge; the line above leads north across the river to Builth Road Station. For a short distance beyond the bridge the path runs parallel with a lane that serves Dolyrerw Farm and Rhosferig Lodge.

The path soon moves away from the lane and continues along the tree lined riverbank, through five fields, until meeting back up with the lane to Rhosferig Lodge.

Penddol Rocks near Builth

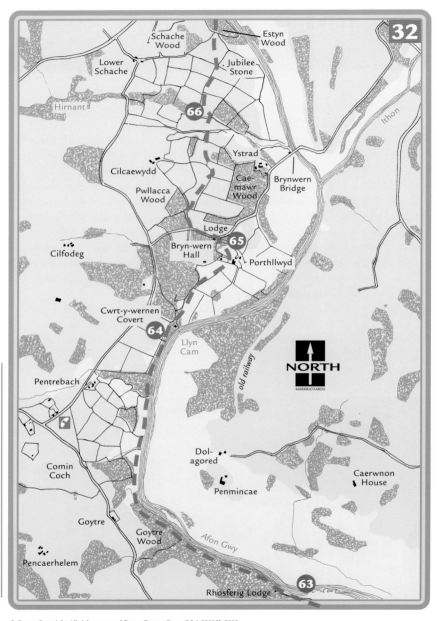

32

Schache Wood

Estyn Wood

Lower Schache

Jubilee Stone

Hirnant

66

Ithon

Ystrad

Cilcaewydd

Cae-mawr Wood

Brynwern Bridge

Pwllacca Wood

Lodge

65

Cilfodeg

Bryn-wern Hall

Porthllwyd

Cwrt-y-wernen Covert

64

Llyn Cam

old railway

ONE MILE

NORTH

MARKRICHARDS

Pentrebach

ONE KILOMETRE

Comin Coch

Dol-agored

Caerwnon House

Penmincae

Goytre

Goytre Wood

Pencaerhelem

Afon Gwy

63

Rhosferig Lodge

Follow the lane ⟨63⟩ straight ahead for a short distance until it drops down closer to the river. Here the walk leaves the track and continues along the riverbank, passing by the private steps on the left up to the lodge. The sloping meadow below the lodge is full of wild flowers in the summer. Take the stile ahead into the first of two fields backed by conifers. In the second field the path runs alongside the river where in places small areas of hardwoods have been planted. At the end of the second field there is a footbridge crossing a small stream beyond which lies Goytre wood. Upon entering the wood keep right to the lower of the two paths available, and follow the riverbank. Within the wood the path stays close to the river, but does climb above it for part of the way, however it drops back down to the river as the path leaves the wood. Keeping to the riverside, the path now

Sheep on a spring day

crosses four fields beyond which the path enters the first of two adjoining conifer plantations, the second of which is quite narrow, with the path generally moving away from and above the river.

64 The path now enters a broadleaved wood, keep to the top edge. The right of way ahead has been diverted so please make sure to follow the waymarks. A fishing lodge is situated at the north edge of the wood on the river side. The path starts to descend in the direction of the lodge but soon bears away from the lodge to the stile in the northwest corner of the wood. Leave the woodland, cross the stream and carry straight on up a slight incline until the field levels out. Now bear left follow the fence line alongside the woodland until the next stile is reached.

Once in the next field, follow the fence on the right and head for the gate across the field, just to the left of the buildings of Porthllwyd Farm. Pass through the gate and continue with the barn to the right and then turn right into the yard and take the first gate on the left. Cross a small field leading to a small piece of woodland beyond which lies a minor road.

65 Turn left on the road and after approximately 150 yards past Bryn-

wern Lodge cross the stile on the right. Head along the field edge alongside Pwllacca Wood and then into the next field. Turn half right and carry on to meet the hedge on the right. Go on to the next gateway, pass through and keep to the hedge on the left. As the hedge starts to turn left towards a gate, leave the hedge line and walk out across the field, to the stile in its corner. Cross the next field to the stile situated in the far fence line. Beyond the stile follow the fence to the next gate, ignore the track here, and in the next field follow the fence on the right to the Hirnant brook.

66 On crossing the footbridge climb straight up the bank to the field and head toward its left-hand corner. In the next two fields follow the hedge on the left, on entering the third field keep half left down the slope towards Estyn Wood and the corner of the field.

Note the Jubilee Stone in the field to the right, that marks the site of a bonfire in 1887 commemorating Queen Victoria's Golden Jubilee.

Pied flycatcher

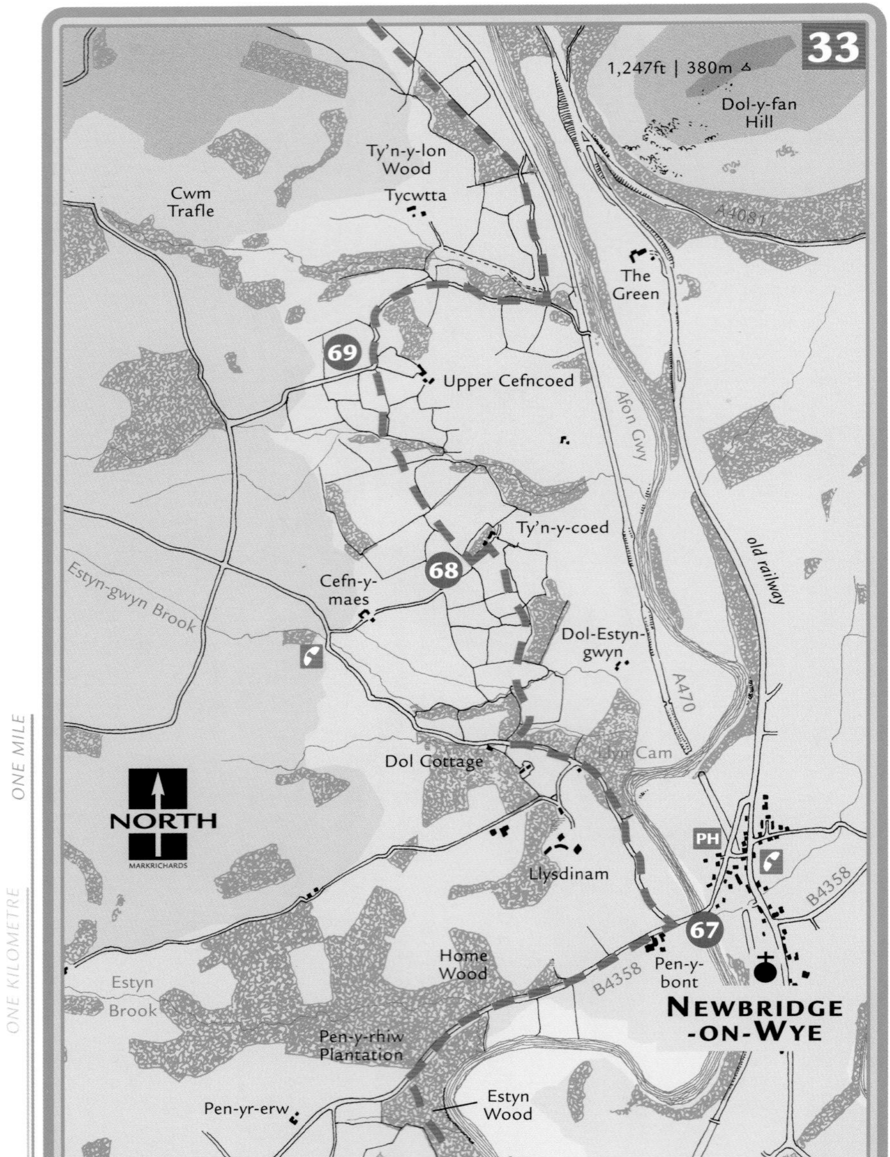
33
1,247ft | 380m
Dol-y-fan Hill
A4081
Ty'n-y-lon Wood
Tycwtta
Cwm Trafle
The Green
69
Upper Cefncoed
Afon Gwy
old railway
Ty'n-y-coed
68
Cefn-y-maes
Estyn-gwyn Brook
Dol-Estyn-gwyn
A470
Llyn Cam
Dol Cottage
NORTH
MARKRICHARDS
PH
Llysdinam
B4358
67
Home Wood
Pen-y-bont
Estyn Brook
B4358
NEWBRIDGE -ON-WYE
Pen-y-rhiw Plantation
Estyn Wood
Pen-yr-erw
ONE MILE
ONE KILOMETRE

33

ESTYN WOOD TO TY'N-Y-LON WOOD

Enter the wood. After a few yards there is a fork in the path. Keep left and carry on, going over a series of 4 boardwalks. Soon, at another fork, take the path to the left that leads to the B4358. Turn right and follow the road towards Newbridge-on-Wye, about ¾ km.

67 Just before reaching the Wye Bridge turn left, opposite Pen-y-bont farm, along a minor road signposted Llysdinam. Go past the entrance to Llysdinam House and, immediately before Dol Cottage on the left, turn right and follow the footpath north.

The route now follows the left hand edge of two fields before it reaches Estyn-gwyn Brook. Cross the footbridge, and then after a short distance through a narrow strip of woodland cross a second footbridge and go into a field. Head for the stile across this field and cross a series of stiles keeping close to the fence line on the right until the track to Ty'n-y-coed is reached. Turn left along the track to the end of Ty'n-y-coed wood, then turn right along the end of the wood and into the next field.

68 Follow the hedge on the left to the far corner of the field, via a section of boardwalk on the way. From the corner of this field pass over a stile and boardwalk across a ditch into the next field. Turn right and carry on to meet the field boundary. Follow this boundary until it turns right. Then head for the stile across the field, and looking toward a dingle ahead, continue diagonally to the left to the fingerpost on the edge of the dingle. The path leads down the dingle and across a footbridge.

Heading back up the slope, turn right along the top of the slope for a short distance to enter the corner of the adjoining field via a stile. Keep close to the hedge line on the right, heading north, via a boardwalk to the minor road.

69 Go straight on and keep on the road until it turns left over a small stone bridge. Continue over the bridge, passing the turn for Tycwtta Farm. The track now becomes unsurfaced and leads to Ty'n-y-lon Wood. Keep to the lower edge of the wood until the track emerges onto the open common.

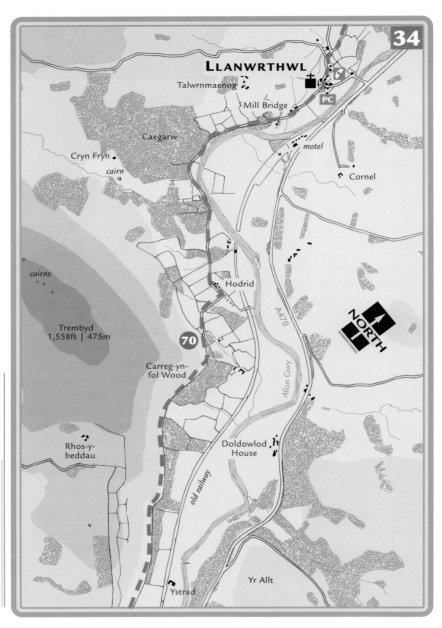

34

TY'N-Y-LON WOOD TO LLANWRTHWL

The route follows the track for $1\frac{1}{4}$ miles. Look out for the occasional glimpses of the River Wye below.

Keep to the track passing two small plantations; fine views can be gained across the valley including Doldowlod House. At the end of the second plantation leave the open hill through a gate and turn left onto a metalled lane.

70 The route now keeps to the lane all the way to Llanwrthwl Village, a distance of $1\frac{1}{2}$ miles. Passing Hodrid House the lane crosses a small section of common. Once past the common the road moves closer to the river,

which can be seen to the right at the base of the wooded slope. Shortly after passing a house on the left, called Craig-Llyn, the road starts to move back a little away from the river, passing an old mill, bridge, and chapel and then carries on to Llanwrthwl.

On entering the village, pass the church on the left, turn left and take the road out of the village. Immediately past the last building on the right, which is the old school, turn right and leave the road at the first bend and keep straight ahead up an old track to meet a minor road at Dolgai Farm.

Cows in the Wye Valley, Powys

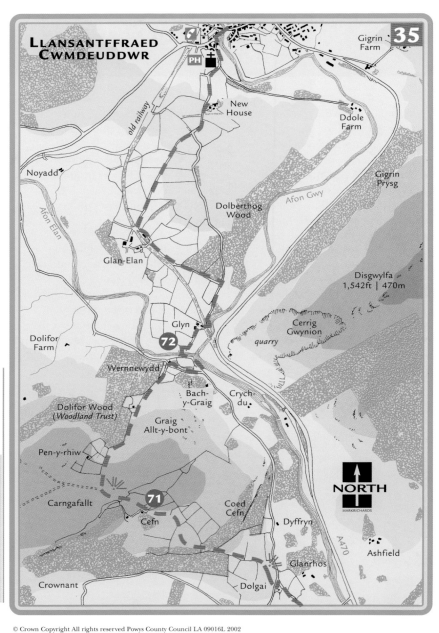

LLANSANTFFRAED CWMDEUDDWR

35

Gigrin Farm

PH

New House

Ddole Farm

old railway

Noyadd

Gigrin Prysg

Afon Gwy

Afon Elan

Dolberthog Wood

Glan-Elan

Disgwylfa
1,542ft | 470m

Glyn

Cerrig Gwynion

quarry

Dolifor Farm

72

Wernnewydd

Bach-y-Graig

Crych-du

Dolifor Wood
(*Woodland Trust*)

Graig
Allt-y-bont

Pen-y-rhiw

NORTH
MARKRICHARDS

Carngafallt

71

Coed Cefn

Cefn

Dyffryn

Ashfield

A470

Glanrhos

Crownant

Dolgai

ONE MILE

ONE KILOMETRE

Turn left along the road for 50 yards and turn right up the farm track. As height is gained so the views of the valley and its surrounding hills become more impressive.

Progressing up the track, it turns left with the right of way here cutting the corner across the field keeping alongside the old wall leading to a gate. Beyond the gate lies Cefn Wood, continue along the track through the wood and across a field to a gateway. The track now becomes more enclosed, passing a small quarry on the right just before reaching Cefn Farm.

71 Pass through the farm yard, making sure to shut the gates, to the field beyond. Once in the field the track splits. Follow the track straight ahead and through the gate. The track now continues across open hill,

Confluence of rivers near Rhayader

called Carngafallt that is an RSPB nature reserve.

The reserve is made up of an undulating mosaic of moorland habitats, including heather, gorse, dry south facing slopes, rocky screes and bogs and pools with cotton grass. Bird life includes linnets and stonechats with snipe and reed bunting in the boggy areas. Dor beetles may be encountered along the stony track often trying to move sheep droppings.

In a short distance the track forks again, turn right here passing Pen-y-rhiw on the left and keeping to the edge of the common, follow the path down the slope. Here, there are extensive views north, across the valley to the old quarry and Gwastedyn Hill, and to Rhayader, with the confluence of the River Elan and River Wye in the foreground.

Dolifor Wood, on the left, is owned by the Woodland Trust and people are invited to walk through it. It contains an unusual mixture of trees - native birch, alder and oak together with more exotic species planted by the former owner.

At the lower edge of the common a narrow lane leads to the minor road. At Wernnewydd House, turn right along the road for 200 yards and take the track on the left. This track leads to the narrow and swaying suspension bridge

across the Elan, at the old fording point just before it joins the River Wye.

72 Once across the bridge turn right and join the lane to The Glyn Farm. On approaching the farm pass through the gate and bear right, continuing on the lane, which soon becomes metalled. Keep to the lane for 400 yards and then turn left along an unsurfaced lane. This lane eventually meets and runs parallel to the old railway line. At the next junction keep right, as turning left here passes under the railway line to Glan-Elan farm. The route now passes between farm buildings to another junction and again here keep right. Please note that the course of the old railway is not a Right of Way.

After turning right, follow the lane for $1/_2$ mile to its junction with a tarmac minor road and continue straight on. This minor road leads to Rhayader, passing the properties of New House Farm on the right and Glanserth on the left. On entering Cwmdeuddwr take a short street to the right leading up to the main road.

An attractive alternative path can be taken, following the fingerpost on the left in front of 'Glanserth', down through Cwmdeuddwr churchyard, bearing right at the main road to the bridge and the centre of Rhayader.

Upper Wye near Rhayader

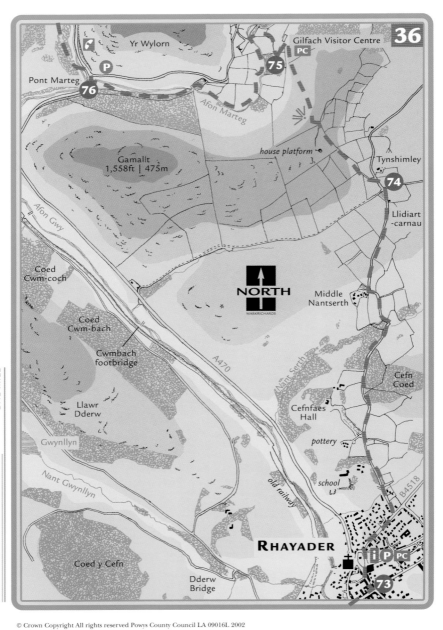

36

Yr Wylorn

Gilfach Visitor Centre
PC

75

P

Pont Marteg

76

Afon Marteg

house platform

Tynshimley

74

Gamallt
1,558ft | 475m

Afon Gwy

Llidiart
-carnau

Coed
Cwm-coch

NORTH

MARKRICHARDS

Middle
Nantserth

Coed
Cwm-bach

A470

Cefn
Coed

Cwmbach
footbridge

Nant Serth

Cefnfaes
Hall

Llawr
Dderw

pottery

Gwynllyn

B4518

Nant Gwynllyn

old railway

school

RHAYADER

i P PC

Coed y Cefn

73

Dderw
Bridge

ONE MILE

ONE KILOMETRE

The route from Rhayader to Llangurig includes sections of high level walking over open countryside. If a lower level alternative is preferred then the quiet, attractive road on the west of the River Wye can be followed between Rhayader and Llangurig.

To continue on the Wye Valley Walk follow the main road into the centre of Rhayader, taking time to look over the bridge at the River Wye.

When the Wye reaches Rhayader it encounters a rocky channel and the resulting waterfall gave the town its proper name of Rhaedr Gwy meaning 'the waterfall of the Wye'. The falls below the bridge are impressive, especially when the river is in spate.

In the past, Rhayader was an important crossroads on the coaching road from Aberystwyth to markets in England. There were turbulent times here in the days of the Rebecca Riots in 1843, but today the town has the reputation of being a friendly place, very welcoming to visitors and with a good selection of accommodation and places to eat.

Rhayader

Gilfach Nature Reserve

73 Turn left at the clock tower in Rhayader and walk along North Street as far as the Leisure Centre and Tourist Information Centre. Turn right on the B4518 signposted to St. Harmon. Stay on the right hand side of the road for about 500 yards before turning left up a minor road, passing the school and pottery workshop.

Carry on uphill and downhill as the road winds through an oak wood and climb past Middle Nantserth Farm. After another ¹/₂ mile, at the crest, a bridleway leaves the road on the right and a footpath on the left. Continue on past these, following the road downhill, and take the next turn on the left, just before Tynshimley, leading onto an enclosed track.

74 Pass through three fields keeping to the right hand edge. To the left,

above the track in the third field are the remains of a house platform. Go straight on along rough hillside with gorse bushes, still keeping the fence line on the right. Pass through a gate leading onto the open hillside. From here there is an excellent view of the Marteg Valley and surrounding hills.

Carry straight on for a few yards and then bear left and shortly turn right following a path heading diagonally down the hillside to Gilfach Nature Reserve, owned and managed by the Radnorshire Wildlife Trust. Ignore the paths leading off to the left, and head down hill towards the farm buildings that can be glimpsed in front of a small stand of conifers.

Lower down the track becomes more obvious and after crossing a stile a made up path leads to the farmyard, which houses a unique Medieval Welsh Longhouse, and, in the barn opposite a visitor centre. Picnic benches and toilets are also available.

4000 years in the making, Gilfach is an old landscape overlooked by a Bronze Age burial mound, with deserted house sites, green lanes and ancient stone walls. This is set within a landscape comprising high moorland, enclosed meadows, oak woodlands and the rocky, tumbling waters of the Afon Marteg. A variety of trails explore the nature reserve.

75 The Wye Valley Walk leaves the farmyard to the left on a metalled lane leading down to the Afon Marteg. Cross over the bridge and turn immediately left following the Nature Trail (waymarked in yellow) along the river bank. *This river section, in part pastoral and in part rocky and dramatic, allows particularly good sightings of*

dippers and grey wagtails. In the summer look out for increasingly scarce Fritillary butterflies, the Bloody-nosed Beetle and Glow-worm. After about ½ mile the trail leaves the river and snakes up to a railway embankment. To the right is a sealed tunnel. *This was part of the old Mid Wales Railway that existed for 99 years and closed in 1962.*

Turn left and follow the course of the old railway back over the river. Carry on, now high above the water, until you see a trail going off to the right shortly before the A470 road. Go down steps and over a footbridge to meet the main road at Pont Marteg.

76 Turn right over the Afon Marteg and carefully cross the A470 to a layby. To the rear of the layby is a path leading down to a footbridge over the River Wye.

Gilfach Longhouse

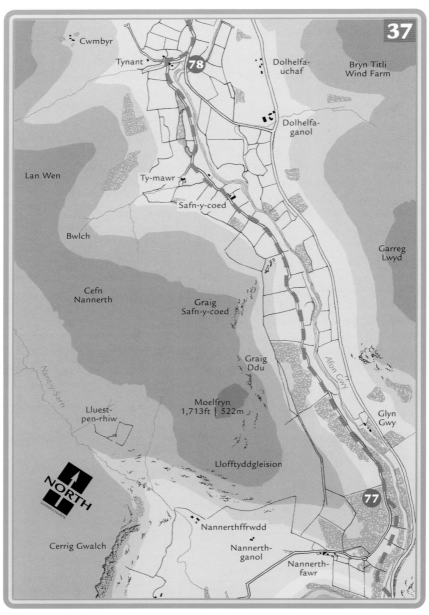

37

Cwmbyr

Tynant **78**

Dolhelfa-uchaf

Bryn Titli Wind Farm

Dolhelfa-ganol

Lan Wen

Ty-mawr

Safn-y-coed

Bwlch

Garreg Lwyd

Cefn Nannerth

Graig Safn-y-coed

Graig Ddu

Afon Gwy

Nant-y-Sarn

Moelfryn 1,713ft | 522m

Lluest-pen-rhiw

Glyn Gwy

Llofftyddgleision

NORTH

77

Nannerthffrwdd

Cerrig Gwalch

Nannerth-ganol

Nannerth-fawr

ONE MILE

ONE KILOMETRE

PONT MARTEG TO DERNOL VALLEY

Cross the bridge and turn right following a path that leads diagonally up through the woodland to a wicket gate. Pass through the gate and continue in the same direction across an open field leading up to a track. Turn right along the track and continue through further fields until a narrow metalled road is joined.

77 Turn right and follow the road along an extremely attractive stretch of the river. Rounded hills line the course of the valley with occasional crags. Follow this gated lane for almost 2 miles passing by Safn-y-coed farm.

On reaching a T junction turn right and at the next junction left. **78**

Near Safn-y-coed Farm

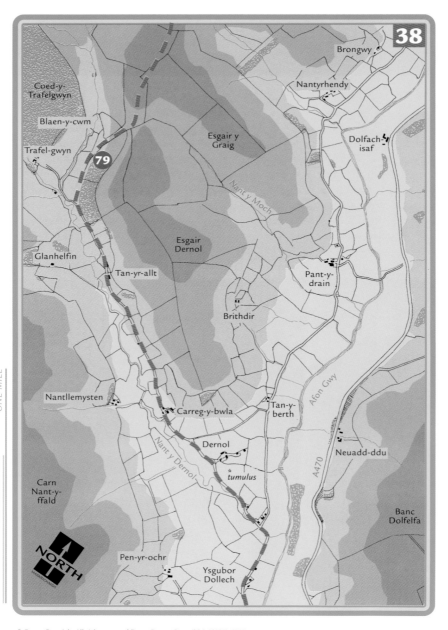

38

Brongwy

Nantyrhendy

Coed-y-
Trafelgwyn

Blaen-y-cwm

Esgair y
Graig

Dolfach
isaf

Trafel-gwyn

79

Nant y Moch

Glanhelfin

Esgair
Dernol

Pant-y-
drain

Tan-yr-allt

Brithdir

Afon Gwy

Nantllemysten

Tan-y-
berth

Carreg-y-bwla

Nant y Dernol

Dernol

Neuadd-ddu

A470

Carn
Nant-y-
ffald

tumulus

Banc
Dolfelfa

NORTH

Pen-yr-ochr

Ysgubor
Dollech

Parts of the next two sections cross high open countryside. If a lower level alternative is preferred, stay on the road to Llangurig.

Carry on for about ½ mile and, as the road to Llangurig swings right, go straight on heading up the Dernol Valley. This is a gated road, so please leave all gates as you find them. Cross two cattle grids and pass the farm Carreg y bwla. The gated road continues up by Tan-yr-allt. A gate at this point is succeeded by another gate after 400 yards. Some 200 yards beyond this, bear right off the road onto the grass track running beneath a birch wood.

79 Approaching the second old hedgeline rising from the valley, branch up right and climb towards a gate leading to an enclosed track going steeply up the mountain side. Climb up through two more gates after which the gradient eases into an open field. Looking back there is a good view of the valley, dominated by the conifers of Coed-y-Trafelgwyn seemingly spilling into the Nant Blaen-y-cwm valley.

Turn half left and cross the field diagonally, passing through an area of marshy land and heading for a stile just to the right of some sheep pens. To the right Bryn Titli wind farm can be seen. Cross the stile and cut the corner of the field to the next stile. Turn right and keeping the fence line on the right go ahead along the ridge-top, gradually veering away from the fence line towards a gate and a stile

Dernol Valley

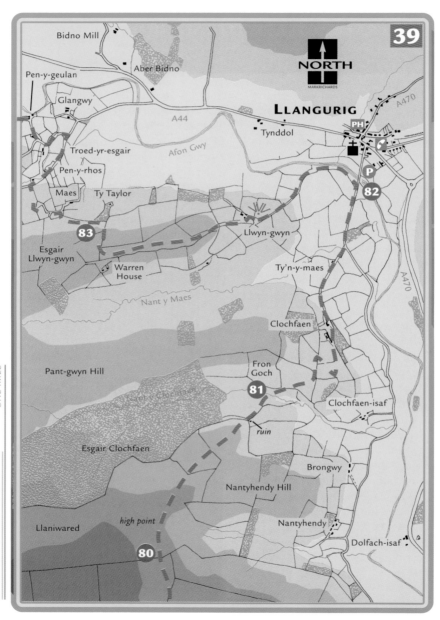

ONE MILE
ONE KILOMETRE

ESGAIR Y GRAIG TO PEN-Y-GEULAN

Plynlimon, source of the River Wye, can now be seen in the distance to the north-west. This gate leads onto open land with a small unnamed summit ahead. At 1575ft this is one of the highest points on the walk.

80 Aim for a point on the right-hand shoulder of the hill, ignoring a track that skirts the left-hand edge.   When adjacent to the summit turn half right and go downhill to a stile at a corner of a field. Go through the next field and cross the stile in the facing fence line.
Carry on in the same direction to reach another stile in the far corner of the field near to a ruin sheltered by a few larch trees. Cross the stile and follow the right-hand field boundary down towards a track that leads to the Nant y Clochfaen ('stream that rings like a bell').

81 Cross the footbridge and follow the track up to join the forestry access track. Go straight over the track and follow the footpath diagonally right up the pasture to reach a gate in the corner . Turn left through the gate and walk ahead with the hedge on the right until an open track crosses the path. Turn right following the track and zigzag down it eventually meeting a narrow metalled road. Bear right down this road passing the buildings of Clochfaen.

Clochfaen is an impressive building. The major part of the present Clochfaen was either built or remodelled in the years 1914-1915 to the designs of William Arthur Smith Benson - a leading figure in the Arts

Llangurig church from route

and Crafts Movement. The house was visited in 1917 by the young Prince Albert, later George VI, who was sent here to recuperate. It was sold in 1927 to the Stirk family, who still retain an interest in the property.

Short walks and viewing points are being developed in the woodland area in front of Clochfaen and these are open to the public.

Carry on along this metalled road until it joins the road leading left into Llangurig. The Wye Valley Walk leaves this road just before the bridge over the river.

It is well worth venturing into the village of Llangurig - the first village on the River Wye. The parish church was founded before 550AD and has some fine woodwork and stained glass windows. There are also a couple of places to obtain refreshments before heading on up the Wye Valley.

82 To continue on the walk turn left before the bridge onto a surfaced road leading uphill to Llwyn-gwyn Farm. The road eventually bears right and approaches the farmyard. Glance down right to see good views of the River Wye below. Turn left, just before entering the farmyard, and skirt around the farm buildings onto a stony farm track. Still climbing, go past two transmitting towers to a pair of gates at the top of the track. Pass

through the left hand gate leading onto more open country.

Continue on, with the gradient soon easing. Down to the left is a small stream, Nant y Maes. Stay on the ridge, leaving the track that goes down to the ruins of Warren House. Carry on for a short distance and then turn right down hill, well before the small wood ahead, to meet a corner in the fence. Follow the track going through two gates and then go down a steep incline to the bottom of the field and turn left alongside a small plantation.

83 Carry on walking with the fence line on the right until a stile is reached. Cross this and follow the fence line down to an old lane. Turn left along the lane passing through a gate and after a few yards bearing diagonally right across the field to reach a stile and small bridge. Turn right in the next field and follow the field boundary down to reach a wide stony forestry access track.

Turn right and continue along the road passing Pen-y-rhos. Turn left at the road junction and follow the road as it loops past Troed-yr-esgair. As the road swings to the left, carry straight on over a cattle grid to a farm track leading down to Pen-y-geulan farm.

View of the Upper Wye

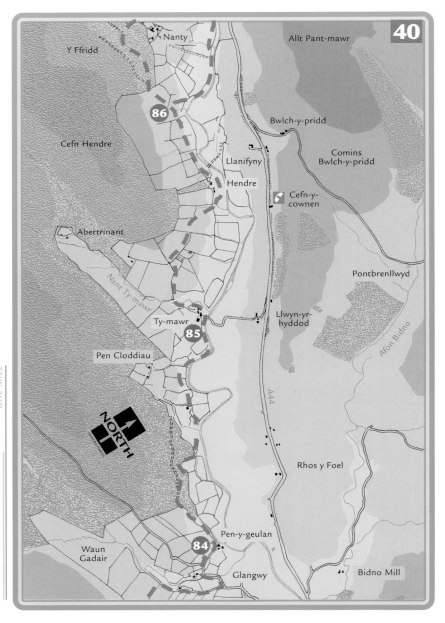

40

Nanty

Y Ffridd

Allt Pant-mawr

86

Cefn Hendre

Bwlch-y-pridd

Comins
Bwlch-y-pridd

Llanifyny

Hendre

Cefn-y-
cownen

Abertrinant

Pontbrenllwyd

Nant Ty-mawr

Ty-mawr

Llwyn-yr-
hyddod

85

Afon Bidno

Pen Cloddiau

A44

NORTH

Rhos y Foel

ONE KILOMETRE   ONE MILE

Pen-y-geulan

84

Waun
Gadair

Glangwy

Bidno Mill

Keeping to the left of and above the farm buildings of Pen-y-geulan **84** follow the track through a gate and over another cattle grid. Continue along the track until a path on the right is marked. This loops down towards the river. The walk now passes through several riverside fields before reaching Ty-mawr farm.

85 The walk follows a track around the edge of Ty-mawr farm, passing a large bridge on the right. The track bears left leaving the River Wye and following the Nant Ty-mawr. Take the right hand fork and cross the stream following the path uphill to a gate. Turn right and follow the track leading downhill, passing an old barn on the way.

At the bottom of this track turn left and almost immediately bear right towards the river bank and a stile. The path loops around in front of Hendre, before crossing the drive and going uphill and crossing a footbridge and stile leading into a field.

Proceed through four fields before reaching a gate. There is a choice of routes at this point, a riverside or woodland option.

86 To follow the riverside path bear right down the hillside towards a gate. Turn left and follow the path that soon leads onto a farm track running near the river. When the track bends sharp left take the stile on the right and follow the river bank to the next stile that leads back into a field with a bridge crossing the Nant-y-Cwm. Continue through further fields to reach a large footbridge over the River Wye. Don't cross this, but follow the top of the flood bank around to reach the forest road.

To follow the higher woodland path bear half left once through the gate and head uphill towards the hedge line. Pass though the hedge line and continue diagonally uphill to reach a gate providing access into the woodland. Turn right and follow the forestry track. At a T junction turn right and cross the Nant y Cwm. At the next fork of tracks keep left and follow the main forestry track. Ignore the next right hand turn down to Nanty. Continue along the track until a turn on the right leads downhill back towards the river and rejoins the riverside route.

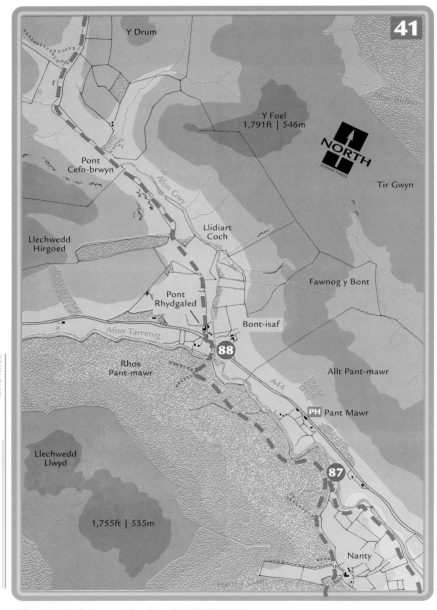

Y Drum

Y Foel
1,791ft | 546m

41

NORTH
MASENICHARDS

Tir Gwyn

Pont
Cefn-brwyn

Afon Gwy

Afon Bidno

Llechwedd
Hirgoed

Llidiart
Coch

Fawnog y Bont

Pont
Rhydgaled

Afon Tarrenig

Bont-isaf

88

Rhos
Pant-mawr

Allt Pant-mawr

A44

PH Pant Mawr

Llechwedd
Llwyd

87

1,755ft | 535m

Nanty

Nant y Cwm

ONE MILE

ONE KILOMETRE

NANTY TO SWEET LAMB

The Wye Valley Walk now continues along this track **87** close to the river. Turn right at the next crossroads and cross the Afon Tarrenig on a footbridge, just before it joins the River Wye.

88 Go up to the A44 at Pont Rhydgaled and cross the road carefully. Turn left and immediately take the entrance on the right leading into a farmyard. Go through the farmyard and climb gently uphill along the broad, stone-surfaced track, with the River Wye down below. As well as a big sheep farm, this is also home of the Sweet Lamb Rally Complex and some major rallying events take place here.

After ³⁄₄ mile cross the river and continue on the main track, passing two roads coming in from the right.

The surrounding land from here upwards is covered with the remains of old mines. Lead and silver mining was a major industry in this area through the 18th and 19th centuries, although there is evidence that lead was mined from here in the Middle Ages and even earlier. Many of the mines eventually shut down in the 1930s. There are old mine shafts around so please keep on the track.

Several flumes and rain gauges are also passed in this area. The Centre of Ecology and Hydrology are undertaking a national research project comparing the Wye and Severn headwaters. Please do not approach or touch the equipment.

Nanty Farm

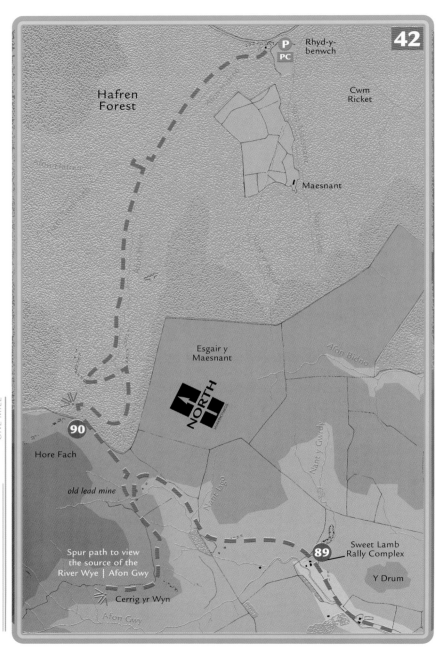

42

Rhyd-y-
benwch

P
PC

Cwm
Ricket

Hafren
Forest

Afon Hafren

Maesnant

Esgair y
Maesnant

Afon Bidno

NORTH

90

Hore Fach

Nant y Gwndy

old lead mine

Nant Iago

Spur path to view
the source of the
River Wye | Afon Gwy

Sweet Lamb
Rally Complex

89

Cerrig yr Wyn

Y Drum

Afon Gwy

ONE MILE

ONE KILOMETRE

Continue on the track towards some stock sheds, ignoring several incoming roads. Pass through gates and continue up the track until a large parking area is reached at the Sweet Lamb Rally Complex.

89 Carry on along the same track through a gate, after which the river bends to the left on the way to its source. There is a good view of the watershed on Plynlimon from here. Go straight on to a gate by a small plantation and climb uphill on the track to a double bend. The valley to the left is black with mining spoil and you can see the remains of an old level running into the hillside. Follow the road bending to the left and then to the right. A track to the left on the second bend leads to a viewing point that offers superb views towards the actual source of the Wye. Well worth the short detour!

Plynlimon is one of the most important upland areas for nature conservation in Wales, particularly for its heathland and birdlife. The main vegetation types are acid grassland, blanket bog and dwarf-shrub heath. Birds of prey seen here include buzzard, kestrel, red kite and peregrine falcon.

Red Kite

The Wye Valley Walk continues climbing up the main track, soon reaching a high point from which the large expanse of Hafren Forest can be seen.

The forest takes its name from Afon Hafren (River Severn) which rises in a deep, blanket-peat bog, 1.25 kilometres outside its boundary, high above, on the slopes of Plynlimon. Once empty but for sheep and derelict lead mines, the renewable forest resource now spans 30 square kilometres. Whilst producing valuable timber for the manufacture of newsprint, chipboard, pallets, fencing and construction timbers, the Forest Enterprise manages the Commissions woodlands for wildlife, archaeological conservation and the quiet enjoyment of visitors.

90 Enter the forest through a gate leading on to a wide forest road. *At the first bend look down to the left to see the remains of Nant yr Eira Mine by the Afon Hore. In the late 19th century 33 tonnes of lead were recovered from the old Bronze Age open cut and more from the many shafts and levels.*

Follow the track downhill along a series of wide sweeping bends to a junction. Turn left and follow the track down to a bridge over the Afon Hore. Turn immediately right and take a stony path that follows the Afon Hore downstream.

This is one of a number of excellent trails that have been developed in the forest, under the co-ordination of Forest Enterprise. The river tumbles through rocks and in about a mile merges with the River Severn (Afon Hafren).

Turn left along the banks of the River Severn and after about 200 yards cross a bridge and join the route of the Severn Way.

The Severn Way is the longest riverside walk in Britain at 210 miles from the source on Plynlimon to the mouth of the Severn at Bristol.

Turn right, once over the bridge, and follow the River Severn along, passing a flume and reaching an area with picnic tables from where a boardwalk continues downstream. At the end of the boardwalk go straight ahead up a surfaced path and zigzag up to Rhyd-y-benwch car park. Here toilets, picnic tables, interesting wooden sculptures and a boulder stone brought from Chepstow, will help you celebrate the end of the Wye Valley Walk! You may have arranged a lift from here, but if not an 8 mile stretch of the Severn Way will take you into the market town of Llanidloes.

Towards the source

ACKNOWLEDGEMENTS

Members of the Ramblers'
Association in Powys helped with
checking and updating the route.

The route was also walked and checked
independently by Mike Wagstaff,
Richard McAllister and John Ebden.

Environment Agency for permission to
reproduce the text on nature
conservation, from their publication
"The River Wye Handbook" The Users
Guide; published by WyeMAG 1997.

Countryside Council for Wales.

Community partners within the
Llandiloes area

Design Stephen Paul Dale 01633 665793
Maps Mark Richards
Print Philtone Litho 0117 9521125
Photography Trevor Hulme; pp4, 14, 17,
19, 22, 23, 26, 29, 39, 41, 45, 51, 57, 65,
66, 67, 69, 73, 75, 99, 107.
T. Hulme (Herefordshire Council);
pp7, 11, 42, 43, 55, 59.
Herefordshire Council; pp61, 71.
Ruth Hargest; pp13, 83, 87, 89, 95, 97,
103, 105, 113, 115, 117, 123.
Wye Valley AONB; pp1, 2, 25, 27, 35,
36, 37.
Andy Neale; pp31.
Ann Duggan; pp53.
Powys County Council; pp81, 91, 109,
119, 127
Radnorshire Wildlife Trust; pp110, 111.
E.P.Powell; pp125
Mike Longridge; Cover